A gift for _____

From _____

Date _____

THERE'S

beauty

IN YOUR

BROKENNESS

90 DEVOTIONS
TO SURRENDER STRIVING, LIVE UNBURDENED,
AND FIND YOUR WORTH IN CHRIST

Brittany Maher &
Cassandra Speer

THOMAS NELSON
Since 1798

There's Beauty in Your Brokenness

Published in Nashville, Tennessee, by Thomas Nelson. Thomas Nelson is a registered trademark of HarperCollins Christian Publishing, Inc.

Published in association with The Bindery Agency, www.TheBinderyAgency.com.

Art © Brittany Maher

Thomas Nelson titles may be purchased in bulk for educational, business, fund-raising, or sales promotional use. For information, please email SpecialMarkets@ThomasNelson.com.

ISBN 978-1-4002-3118-8 (audiobook)
ISBN 978-1-4002-3116-4 (eBook)
ISBN 978-1-4002-3119-5 (HC)

Printed in Malaysia

23 24 25 26 27 OFF 10 9 8 7 6 5 4 3 2 1

Contents

your worth
is not
up for
grabs

Living from Worth, Not for It

God created mankind in his own image, in the image of God
he created them; male and female he created them.

GENESIS 1:27

O
ne of the biggest lies that humanity has bought into is that our worth is earned—and it can be revoked if we mess up or don't measure up.

Sister, I have good news for you. Absolutely none of that is true! But let's take a step back. Where did that lie come from in the first place? You guessed it: the Enemy of our souls, who will stop at nothing to convince us that we're not worthy of the space we take up in this world. And once we've bought into his lies, he'll send us on a fruitless mission to "find ourselves" in all the wrong places.

Listen, we get it: those lies are convincing, aren't they? When you scroll through social media posts of friends buying a brand-new house that's way out of your price range, going on fabulous trips you've only dreamed of, or parenting children who are smart and sweet and staying ahead of the curve, it's hard not to look at your own life and think, *How much more do I need to do to be the woman, the wife, the mom I'm supposed to be?* Or maybe you've messed up. Maybe it feels like your mistake took the life God had planned for you and snatched it right out of His hand. Now nothing will ever be good again.

Those moments can feel so hard, right?

But don't forget: you're *not* who the world, the Enemy, or *anybody* says you are. You are who God says you are. And here's what He says about you: sweet friend, you are God's masterpiece (Ephesians 2:10 NLT), made in His own image and likeness (Genesis 1:27). Let that sink in for a moment. You bear the image of the Creator. No wonder the Enemy wants to make it so hard to embrace this truth! If the Enemy can convince you to chase after your worth in all the wrong places, then he can keep you from discovering who you truly are in Christ.

Remember, the God whose hands created the universe also carefully knit you together within your mother's womb (Psalm 139:13). He knows the number of stars in the sky (Psalm 147:4) and counted every strand of hair on your head (Luke 12:7). You are so precious in His sight. You are the daughter of the Most High. No matter what you've done, know this to be true: God loves you. And nothing you ever do could separate you from His love (Romans 8:38–39).

So don't let the devil lie to you. Live secure in this soul-anchoring truth: your worth isn't up for grabs—your Creator already secured it. Today's a great day to start living *from* worth instead of *for* it.

Cass

God Delights in the Details

The LORD directs the steps of the godly. He delights in
every detail of their lives. Though they stumble, they
will never fall, for the LORD holds them by the hand.

PSALM 37:23-24 NLT

I've found so much purpose in motherhood. My daughter is one, and life is so fun with her. She's starting to say a few words now, running around the house, acting silly, and giving the best snuggles.

Yet, as is the case with many blessings, there are also challenges. Motherhood certainly has stretched me far beyond my comfort zone: the tantrums, the late nights from teething, the sick days, the mess that always seems to be there. It's all hard work, but very worthy work.

At times I find myself longing to have just a day to spend in God's presence in total silence and peace away from the chaos that is motherhood, yet it's hard to get away for long stretches of time. I struggle with guilt for having only twenty minutes to sit and read my Bible before my little one is climbing on my lap, needing my attention. The continual start/stop flow of my day can sometimes leave me feeling like it's impossible to accomplish anything, let alone have time to spend with God.

What the Lord has taught me in the midst of my fast-paced days is that He's just as with me in the quiet moments as He is in the busyness, the hurry, the mess.

He is also with me in the small details. Even in the mundaneness of my day, each moment can be a moment spent with God if I press into His presence. From making my cup of coffee in the morning to cleaning up the mess my child just made, He is with me in it all. And there's not a moment wasted when it's a moment spent with Him.

It's the same with you, friend. He delights in every detail of your day, even the details that seem minuscule. They all matter, and they matter to Him.

Britt

Each moment can be a moment spent with God if I press into His presence.

His Plan > Our Failures

Many are the plans in a person's heart, but it
is the Lord's purpose that prevails.

PROVERBS 19:21

*H*ave you ever made a huge mistake you wish you could take back? Or committed such a massive moral failure that you wonder if you ruined God's plan for your life? Maybe someone told you that you're too far gone or too hopeless a cause. If so, you're in good company. There are plenty of mess-ups and misfits in the pages of the Bible.

Abraham was liar, yet God chose him to be the father of many nations.

Moses was a murderer with a stutter, yet God chose him to deliver the Israelites from slavery and out of Egypt.

Rahab was a sex worker, yet she's included in the lineage of Jesus.

Gideon was a coward, yet God used him to lead His army to victory.

Samson was a violent womanizer, yet God used his strength to weaken the Philistine army.

David was an adulterer who abused his position of power, yet he's known as a man after God's own heart.

The Samaritan woman was a disgraced divorcée, yet Jesus revealed

Himself to her as the Messiah. As a result, she became the first recorded evangelist, and many Samaritans came to know Christ through her testimony.

Sweet sister, there's nothing you could possibly do that could disqualify you from the love of God. You're not capable of messing up God's purpose for your life. Rest in this truth: His plan is always greater than your failures. Always.

Cass

There's nothing you could possibly do that could disqualify you from the love of God.

I Used to Be Afraid to Be Seen

"The Lord bless you and keep you; the Lord make his
face shine on you and be gracious to you; the Lord
turn his face toward you and give you peace."

NUMBERS 6:24-26

I have a confession to make. I used to hide from being around people because I was in such a deep state of insecurity, I couldn't handle being in a situation where I'd be seen. Just the thought of others seeing me not at my best gave me immense anxiety.

When my husband started a remote position with an organization that's based out of state, we traveled for a visit to the home office, where we were invited to a dinner with a few executives. I couldn't bring myself to be put in a situation where I'd have to talk to people because at the time, I was so insecure about who I was.

So there I sat in the hotel room alone, hiding. While my husband went and met some amazing people from his new workplace, I missed out. Looking back now, I feel sad that I allowed myself to become so entangled in my insecurity that I couldn't step outside of myself, outside of my comfort zone to be there for my husband. I was so fixated on myself and my own discomfort that I had abandoned him.

I'm sure my husband didn't view it that way. He's loved me

through all my insecurities. But I felt guilt and shame that I allowed my insecurities to rule me.

Not only was I afraid to be seen, but I was afraid of the people around me and their opinions of me. Yet God's Word specifically says two things that relate to this deep-seated fear:

1. "Am I now seeking the approval of man, or of God? Or am I trying to please man? If I were still trying to please man, I would not be a servant of Christ" (Galatians 1:10 ESV).
2. "The fear of the LORD is the beginning of wisdom, and the knowledge of the Holy One is insight" (Proverbs 9:10 ESV).

These verses really helped me through my personal battle of insecurity. If I'm placing the Lord first in my life, then my need to please Him comes before anyone else.

I don't know about you, but I find freedom and rest in that truth. To aim to please God before man gives me a sense of relief because I know that even if I mess up, God will never change His mind about me. The same goes for you, friend.

If you're struggling with feelings of inadequacy or insecurity, know this: God created you and knows every detail about you. He sees every flaw, every insecurity, and every mistake, yet He still loves you the same because His love is unwavering.

So step out of hiding. Let His light shine on you so that it can reflect on others.

Britt

HE IS IN THE SOIL
JUST AS MUCH AS HE
IS IN THE GROWTH.
IF THE SOIL IS GOOD,
THE GROWTH WILL COME.

5

Surviving the Storms of Life

He [Jesus] got up, rebuked the wind, and said to the sea, "Silence!
Be still!" The wind ceased, and there was a great calm.

MARK 4:39 CSB

I woke up at 4:30 in the pitch-black morning to the sound of sirens blaring. I live in Oklahoma, where tornados strike swiftly and sometimes without warning. The violent storm had passed, and dawn was quickly approaching, but my anxiety remained. My heart continued to pound in my chest like the thunder that shook our house.

There will always be literal and metaphorical storms that collide with our lives without warning. Like meteorologists, we work diligently to predict these storms. Sometimes we can recognize the patterns of an impending disaster and seek shelter, but that's not always the case.

When such difficulties arise, remember: not all storms come to disrupt your life. Some storms come to clear your path, water your soil, and strengthen your faith. Sweet friend, when you ask God to help you grow, don't be surprised when it starts to rain.

In Mark 4:35–39, we get a peek into Jesus' humanity. Just as He finished teaching the multitude from the shores of the Sea of Galilee, Jesus and the disciples began to cross the sea by boat. Exhausted, Jesus fell asleep. As He rested, a violent storm formed, and waves began to crash into the boat. Certain they were in danger, the disciples cried out for Jesus to help them. Jesus awakened and rebuked the wind, telling the storm to hush (Mark 4:39). In an instant the wind died down, and it was completely calm.

He is our refuge when we need to seek shelter (Psalm 46:1), but Jesus didn't come just to calm the storms of our lives. No, friend. He is with us as we weather the storms that we wish would pass. If He doesn't silence the wind and the waves that surround you, perhaps there's a storm within your heart He's trying to calm.

If you find yourself overwhelmed by the difficulties of life today, cry out to Jesus. He is our ever-present help in times of trouble.

Cass

When you ask God to help you grow, don't be surprised when it starts to rain.

6

The Clothing Store I Didn't Belong In

God does not show favoritism.

ROMANS 2:11

The bell rang after sixth period was over, and I was pumped to go to the mall with my friends. As a freshman in high school, I was eager to go shopping and get some new outfits for the school year.

While we were trotting through the mall, I saw a reddish-pink sign out of the corner of my eye as I heard one friend shout, "5–7–9! Oh my gosh, we *have* to go in there!"

I hadn't heard of this store before and thought *5–7–9* must've been an area code or something. But it wasn't an area code—oh, no. It was a brand name that described the only Juniors clothing sizes they kept in the store. So me and my size-12 self were obviously bummed when I realized nothing would fit me.

I can still remember how my friends tried on clothes and complimented each other on how great they looked while I stood back in white-hot embarrassment. It was awful. And as we walked out of the store, I saw the glaring reddish-pink 5–7–9 sign one last time. It was a harsh reminder that I didn't belong.

After leaving, I couldn't stop thinking about the painful truth that

I wasn't able to fit into anything at a store that was basically only for skinny girls. For years after, 5–7–9 became a representation of how out of shape I thought I was and how, in order for me to be considered "skinny," I'd have to become one of those sizes.

But here's a truth I wish I would've known at the time, even after losing weight to "belong" in that store: even if a clothing store, or any other place, is exclusive, the kingdom of God and God Himself are inclusive. He does not exclude based on gender, size, occupation, or mistakes. In His kingdom, *all* are welcome. And what we look like has no impact or bearing on His love for us.

Britt

In His kingdom, all are welcome.

7

You Don't Need
Permission to Rest

"Come to me, all you who are weary and burdened, and I will give
you rest. Take my yoke upon you and learn from me, for I am
gentle and humble in heart, and you will find rest for your souls."
MATTHEW 11:28-29

It was another night when I found myself wearily limping my way
to the bedtime finish line. After rushing the kids through our
nighttime routine and tucking my three tiny humans swiftly into bed,
I collected an armful of candles and carried them to my bathroom.
I ran myself a hot bath, turned on a peaceful playlist, and poured a
copious amount of my favorite scented bubbles and Epsom salt into
the tub. As I slowly eased myself into the warm water, I heard the
pitter-patter of little feet scurrying toward me. I felt my body tense as
I braced myself for impact.

My two daughters quietly peeked their heads into the doorway.
"It smells good in here, Mommy. Why are you sitting in the dark?"
my oldest daughter asked.

"Sometimes Mommy likes to light candles and take a relaxing
bath at night," I replied.

"But why?" my youngest daughter responded.

"Because I can."

This answer seemed to quench their curiosity, and they quickly scampered back to bed.

How often do we feel the need to justify giving ourselves permission to rest? Jesus Himself offers us rest and compassion without conditions. Perhaps it's time that we take Him up on His offer. Because when we're weary and heavy-laden, Christ says we can find rest in Him.

Sweet sister, you don't have to earn the right to pause and recharge. God is inviting you to find rest for your weary soul.

Cass

Jesus Himself offers us rest and compassion without conditions.

God Wants to Connect with You

Jesus often withdrew to lonely places and prayed.

LUKE 5:16

Isn't it amazing that we have the opportunity to intimately know the One who created us?

When I think of the word *intimacy*, I'm reminded that it's the deepest level of connection. And the reality is, God wants this connection with us. He desires intimacy and a real relationship with us.

In John 17:3, we're reminded that we're called to know Him—not just to know facts about Him or hear about Him, but to know Him on a deep level. Through intimacy, we have a beautiful chance to understand and know the God we worship and love, to connect our hearts to His will and align our desires with His.

I often get asked what it looks like to spend time with God, and I want to start by saying that Jesus set the perfect example for us: He frequently withdrew to solitary places to pray and talk with His Father.

Jesus understood the importance of being quiet and still before His Father, and He took time away from everyone and everything around Him to make it happen. He tuned out every distraction by going into deserted places to tune in to God's voice, power, and will.

If you desire a deeper connection with God, here are some practices that'll help you develop a deeper intimacy with Him.

- Read His Word every day in a place of solitude.
- Communicate your thankfulness for everything He's blessed you with.
- Turn on some praise music, and pour your heart out to Him through worship.
- Ask Him to reveal to you His will and His heart.
- Ask Him to show you the areas of your life in which you need to release your own grip and surrender to Him.
- Pray that He'll show you any unconfessed sin that you may not see in yourself.
- Spend time in the stillness, just listening. Sometimes we have so many requests to bring *to* Him, we forget to actually take the time to be quiet and listen *for* Him.

Britt

God desires intimacy and a real relationship with us.

9

Our Secrets Make Us Sick

"Nothing is concealed that won't be revealed, and nothing
hidden that won't be made known and brought to light."
LUKE 8:17 CSB

I squirmed in my chair and felt my cheeks flush with heat as I listened to my therapist say, "Our secrets keep us sick."

She paused.

"What we don't deal with in the daylight will deal with us at night."

There it was in my therapist's dimly lit room, the uncomfortable yet undeniable truth I'd been reading in Scripture for years: "Nothing is concealed that won't be revealed, and nothing hidden that won't be made known and brought to light" (Luke 8:17 CSB).

In that moment, I realized the secrets I'd spent most of my life trying to keep were ultimately keeping me sick—physically, mentally, and spiritually. That jives with something that many trauma therapists say: "The body keeps the score," meaning, the moments of fear and devastation that you cannot or will not process are going to show up in your physical or mental health in one way or another.

I've seen this in my own life. When I tried to hide the trauma of my past, I had unintentionally given that trauma free residence in my mind and permission to wreak havoc on my physical and mental health. Panic would sweep over my body every time I heard a loud noise. Something as simple as hearing a heavy door or cabinet slam would physically startle me, causing my breath to quicken and my heart to pound. This hypervigilance and response to my surroundings was a symptom of the complex trauma I had experienced in my past. I worked hard to repress these traumatic experiences, which only intensified my general belief that the world wasn't a safe place and that danger was lurking around every corner. What I once thought was a quirk in my personality I now recognize as a symptom of post-traumatic stress disorder (PTSD). I used to think that something was wrong with me, but I'm now able to acknowledge that something very wrong happened to me.

Over time, after years of therapy, I've seen that avoidance doesn't conceal darkness: it insulates it. Death and destruction flourish when we don't let in the light of connection with our loved ones and our Creator.

Sweet friend, I'm not sure what kind of trauma you're struggling with today, whether you did something you regret or something regrettable happened to you. But what I do know is this: God has never lost sight of you. There's no secret you could confess to Him that He doesn't already know—and He's never stopped loving you through it all. Whatever secret you're carrying, it's time to bring it into the light and stop allowing the darkness to hide you away. What a comfort to know that God can heal the pain of our past and release us from the grip of our secret shame in Jesus' name.

Cass

do it all
unto Him.

When You're Feeling Overwhelmed and Overworked

Whatever you do, work at it with all your heart, as
working for the Lord, not for human masters, since you
know that you will receive an inheritance from the Lord
as a reward. It is the Lord Christ you are serving.

COLOSSIANS 3:23-24

*W*hen I was eighteen years old and newly saved, I was working
at a restaurant as a waitress. Some days I would work double
shifts and be on my feet for fifteen hours a day.

The owner of this restaurant was a rather crabby individual and had
a tendency to overwork his employees. One night after working a double
shift, I was so exhausted that my legs and feet were *throbbing*. All I wanted
to do was sit, but I had to do my cleaning tasks at the end of the night.

As I replenished the salt and pepper, refilled the ketchup bottles,
and cleaned the booths until they were spotless for the next day's
customers, I wondered to myself, *Does my boss even see me working this
hard? Does he even care?*

As I picked up a broom and began sweeping, I felt the Lord speak
to my heart: "I see you. Work as though you are working unto Me.
I'm with you always."

I paused as I remembered Colossians 3:23.

Standing on the floor of the restaurant—exhausted, in pain, and feeling underappreciated—I welled up in tears knowing that Jesus saw me and was proud of my efforts.

Sometimes we get so caught up in thinking that our hard work is canceled out when nobody sees it. But nothing is hidden from the Lord. He sees it all. And when we do it all unto Him, we eliminate our desire to work to be seen and appreciated because we already know we have the greatest reward in Christ. No paycheck or pat on the back could ever replace the inheritance we have in Jesus.

He sees you going above and beyond, friend. He sees your hard work. It doesn't go unnoticed by Him.

Britt

No paycheck or pat on the back could ever replace the inheritance we have in Jesus.

A Snake in the Road

Be sober-minded, be alert. Your adversary the devil is prowling
around like a roaring lion, looking for anyone he can devour.

1 PETER 5:8 csb

*O*ur new neighborhood looks like someone pulled it right out of
a storybook. It has willow trees that drape over ponds, winding
trails that weave through the landscape, and classic streetlamps that
make me think I've landed in Narnia. It's perfect for a relaxing stroll
at twilight.

There's something deeply spiritual about the Oklahoma sunsets.
It feels like God's painting His love on a new canvas each night, and
they are so beautiful that I can get distracted and lose sight of the path
in front of me.

That's exactly what happened a few days ago when I brought my
littles on my evening walk. We were skipping, laughing, and taking
pictures of the sky when suddenly I realized there was a *huge* snake in
the road just a few steps away.

I froze and ordered my children to stay close. As I looked closer,
I noticed the snake's body had been run over, but its head and tail
were still moving vigorously. It was injured, but it was still alive—and
ready to strike.

Later that night, when my adrenaline died down, I couldn't help

23

but think that snake was like the Enemy of our souls: defeated but ready to attack. The devil is smart, and we have to remain alert and keep watch for the things he'll put in our paths to trip us up.

Just as a mother guards her children from danger, there is safety found in proximity to our God. Walk closely with God today—and remain alert to the devil's schemes.

Cass

Just as a mother guards her children from danger, there is safety found in proximity to our God.

_12_

Make the Hustle Healthy

The LORD replied, "My Presence will go with
you, and I will give you rest."

EXODUS 33:14

O ur culture is loaded with messages that encourage us to dream big, set audacious goals, and accomplish great things. It also shows us that working hard now means living burned-out, exhausted, and unsatisfied because accomplishment is the only evidence of worth in this world.

Wow, how we have wandered from God's design of what hard work should look like! We've become so inundated with a hustle mentality that we've forgotten how to surrender our hearts in partnership with God and His plan.

The allure of hustling can be sneaky because, on one hand, it implies action. The grit of a "get 'er done" attitude can motivate us to blast through our task lists, but it shouldn't be the only mindset we live by because if that's the case, then we are only at peace when we're accomplishing something.

I love to move forward with my goals. But in my quest to work hard, I need to make sure my goals are aligned with His will and His plan.

In Galatians 1:10 Paul asked, "Am I now trying to win the approval of human beings, or of God?" To be honest, I have to push myself to reflect on this verse daily because I've spent many years and tears pleasing the ones around me. There are so many seasons when I've allowed my accomplishments to speak higher of my value than Christ.

Friend, you can hustle in a healthy way. Working hard doesn't have to mean you live burned-out. You *can* have one without the other. You *can* function from a place of rest as you remember this truth: you are valuable to God no matter how much you've accomplished.

Britt

You can hustle in a healthy way.

the old life
has gone,
the new life
has come.

13

You're Not Beyond Repair

If anyone is in Christ, the new creation has
come: The old has gone, the new is here!

2 CORINTHIANS 5:17

I'm slightly obsessed with a TV show you might be familiar with called *Fixer Upper*. Maybe you've heard of it? Chip and Joanna Gaines, a lovable and creative couple, help their clients renovate dream homes from houses that often appear broken beyond repair. With a little bit of elbow grease and a whole lot of artistic vision, these homes become something new entirely!

I don't know why, but I've always been enamored with lost causes, even when they're houses that belong to people I don't know. It might sound weird, but I can't help but feel a connection to these homes because I feel like *I'm* under construction too. I can relate to the concept of feeling like my life is a fixer-upper.

I can see myself in these abandoned buildings and neglected interiors. I, too, know what it's like to endure brutal storms, and I've also been weathered by the hardships of life. I've often felt like I'm a lost cause. Maybe you can relate?

The wonderful thing about the gospel is that God doesn't care about our exterior. He doesn't look at the things that the world looks at to determine our value. He looks at the heart. And with

God there are no lost causes; He always leaves us better than He found us.

Here's what I know to be true: you're not broken beyond repair. God is faithful to complete the work He's started (Philippians 1:6), and He isn't finished with you yet!

I hate to be cheesy, but this story of restoring the ruins of these broken homes has the gospel written all over it. In his second letter to the church at Corinth, the apostle Paul wrote, "If anyone is in Christ, the new creation has come: The old has gone, the new is here!" (2 Corinthians 5:17). Oh, what marvelous hope we have in this truth! Our hearts are the ultimate fixer-upper. I can just imagine watching the glorious demolition of all the walls we've built within our hearts— the Lord's careful hands, sanding down our calloused hearts, skillfully removing our rough exteriors, and revealing something totally new in the process.

The truth is, the suffering we've endured in this life has left many of us worn down and in need of repair, but in the deepest depths of our brokenness, Jesus meets us there. He sees our rough exteriors and cracked foundations and calls us to build our lives upon Him, a firm foundation that will endure the test of time and weather any storm life throws at us.

Maybe you've found yourself wondering if you're a lost cause. Maybe someone in your life has convinced you that you're broken beyond repair. Jesus can restore the ruins of your life and transform what was broken into something totally new. I know this to be true. And if it's true for me, it's true for you too.

Cass

14

Walking the Walk,
Even If It's Alone

"If the world hates you, keep in mind that it hated me first.
If you belonged to the world, it would love you as its own.
As it is, you do not belong to the world, but I have chosen
you out of the world. That is why the world hates you."

JOHN 15:18-19

As followers of Jesus, we know it can be difficult sometimes to follow Him in a world that doesn't. When we walk with Christ, it will not make sense to the people around us who are of the world. That's why it's so important for us to be *in* the world, not *of* it.

You see, what God is doing in and through your life is far more important than how it looks to observers from afar. Some people might think you're a little crazy for being involved with this whole "Jesus" thing.

God's purpose for your life is still the same, even if the crowd has left you, even if everyone has turned their backs on you. Your God-given purpose, value, and identity do not waver along with their changing feelings about you.

Noah built the ark and prepared it trusting that God would bring the animals and the flood. Yet he didn't allow outside opinions to deter him from continuing with the assignment God had given him. He placed unwavering trust and hope in God and knew that even if he did it alone, he would still obey Him.

You don't need the largest following or the biggest platform to live out the calling He's placed on your life. You also don't need the approval of the world to live a holy, sanctified life in Christ.

Follow Jesus, even if you're following Him alone in your workplace, your friend group, or your family. You don't need their yes or their approval to follow Jesus. Show them who Jesus is by the loving way you live your life. I know it's hard, especially when you feel alone, but their rejection doesn't change your acceptance by the Father through Christ. You have so much more in Him than you could ever have had without Him.

Britt

God's purpose for your life is still the same, even if the crowd has left you.

15

It's Not Weak to Ask for Help

I lift up my eyes to the mountains—where does my help come from?
My help comes from the Lord, the Maker of heaven and earth.

PSALM 121:1-2

Have you ever been in an overwhelming situation and in need of rescue? Not to be dramatic, but that was totally me recently.

I had just returned to Oklahoma City after an exciting work trip in Nashville, Tennessee, to celebrate our first book launch (!). It was an incredible trip, jam-packed with radio, TV, and podcast interviews. I was overwhelmed with gratitude and excitement, but when I arrived home, a different type of overwhelm began to settle in.

Here's where I need to tell you something: I battle mild anxiety. And under extreme circumstances, I even suffer from debilitating panic attacks.

On even ordinary days, life can feel like a lot. I'm a mother of three who works from home, and our closest family lives six hours away. But on this particular day, my rowdy little humans were home for summer break. I had overlapping projects, multiple deadlines, tons of meetings, and the mission of motherhood all demanding my attention at the same time. The word *overwhelmed* doesn't begin to capture how I felt.

Feeling the tension of my limitations, I reached out for help. But the people I usually look to were unavailable, and I didn't want to inconvenience anyone or let anyone down. I was stretched thin and growing weary. I needed help, but I felt like I was out of options.

And then I felt it starting. My heart began pounding so hard I thought it might burst out of my chest. Before I knew it, I was gasping for air, and my entire body felt like it was on fire.

I slowly walked into the living room, where my husband was relaxing. He glanced up at me with immediate concern and asked what was wrong, but I couldn't get the words out as tears streamed down my face.

"Take a deep breath in through your nose, and slowly let it out from your mouth," he said calmly.

As I inhaled, I placed my hand on my belly, and as I exhaled, I placed my other hand on my chest. I continued to do this until my panic subsided, and I was able to share my concerns with my husband. We talked through a plan to ease the stress I was dealing with. I also sent a text to my closest friends, letting them know what I was going through, and they lovingly rallied around me with prayer.

I wish I could tell you that my anxiety instantly disappeared and my plate became easier to manage, but that simply wasn't true. Life often hands us more than we can handle. The good news is, we don't have to tackle the troubles of this life on our own. God places people in our lives to come alongside us, to bear our burdens with us.

Dear friend, asking for help isn't a sign of weakness; it's proof of wisdom. Allow the people in your life to meet you in your time of need.

So if you're in need of some help, cry out to Him today. He is with you and for you, and He'll provide you what—and who—you need in your overwhelming moments.

Cass

16

Feeling Lame Without the Likes

Fearing people is a dangerous trap, but
trusting the LORD means safety.
PROVERBS 29:25 NLT

I used to purchase likes for my Instagram photos.

It all started when I posted a selfie on my personal Instagram and was mortified to see my photo had received only five likes. It was my favorite selfie, so I didn't want to take it down. I had come across an app through which you could purchase one hundred likes for one dollar, and it seemed like a great bargain to spend only a dollar for people to see I was admired and liked by others.

What I didn't realize at the time was that I was essentially purchasing a stamp of approval of myself for others to see.

I'm relieved to admit that I don't purchase likes anymore, but I do know that apps like the one I used still exist. And the fact that they exist tells us that so many others like me have fallen victim to believing they are worthy only if they have likes. And when our worth rises and falls with the opinions of others, we'll never truly know who we are.

What a lie and trap of the Enemy: that we are only loved, valued, and worthy if we have plenty of likes, followers, and subscribers. As my coauthor, Cass, says, "The devil is all up in the digital details."

The truth is that through Christ, we are approved by God. He doesn't just like us—He loves us with an everlasting love that is irrevocable. He will never change His mind about us.

I went from viewing myself as lame without likes to a royal daughter of God. The same is true for you, friend. You don't need the world's proof that you are worthy, loved, and valued. Christ has already bought your worth.

Britt

When our worth rises and falls with the opinions of others, we'll never truly know who we are.

PERHAPS OUR TEARS ARE FALLING UPON THE SOIL OF THAT WHICH GOD WISHES TO GROW WITHIN US.

You Have to Feel It to Heal It

Those who sow with tears will reap with songs of joy.
Those who go out weeping, carrying seed to sow, will
return with songs of joy, carrying sheaves with them.

PSALM 126:5-6

I've recently been walking through a long season of heartache. I lost two loved ones suddenly, within months of each other. Two of my closest friends have been on the verge of forfeiting their battles with severe depression. The world around me seems to be collapsing under the weight of constant tragedy and violence.

And somehow, in the midst of it all, I've been working on two books based on the concept of true worth and inherent value found in Jesus Christ. What a tension I've been living in, carrying hope in one hand and heartache in the other.

Surrounded by so much grief, I've struggled with allowing myself to surrender to sorrow. Sometimes it can feel like sadness threatens to swallow me whole, and I fight hard for any semblance of control.

Usually when huge waves of heartache come my way, my first response has always been to numb my pain, turning to sleep as a method of escape and the convenience of Chick-fil-A for comfort—always upsizing the fries, of course. Here's the thing: rest and food are necessary and good things. I often joke that Chick-fil-A is the Lord's chicken! But too much of a good thing can become harmful to both our health and our spiritual well-being. I've used these coping mechanisms my whole life, thinking they were the safest route for handling my feelings. I believed that if I allowed myself to let it all out, the tears might never stop.

Thanks to therapy and prayer, here's what I've learned: if we want God to heal it, we must be willing to feel it. Ignoring heartache doesn't make us immune to it; it makes us numb to it.

Psalm 126:5–6 beautifully illustrates the connection between heartache and hope. We cannot celebrate the harvest without the seasons of sowing, toil, and tears. The psalmist invited us to consider that perhaps our tears are falling on the soil that God will use to grow us.

If you find yourself in a season of sorrow and feel tempted to hold it all in . . . just let it out. Not only is a good cry cleansing for the soul, but it's scientifically proven to be good for your physical health. Tears release oxytocin and endorphins, and these feel-good chemicals help ease both physical and emotional pain.[1]

Sometimes in the middle of your grief it's hard to see how God can use your tears. I've been there, and so have many others in the Bible. Hagar sobbed in the wilderness, and God heard her plea (Genesis 21:17). David moaned and groaned to the point of physical exhaustion, yet God heard him and didn't tire of his tears (Psalm 6:6). Jesus wept, even though He knew He'd resurrect His dear friend Lazarus from the grave (John 11:35). Do you see a pattern here? The God of all comfort was with every single one of them, and He's with you too.

Sweet friend, your suffering is seen. If you're living in the tension of carrying hope in one hand and heartache in the other, rest in this truth: God is carrying you right at this very moment.

Cass

Immeasurably More

Now to him who is able to do immeasurably more than all
we ask or imagine, according to his power that is at work
within us, to him be glory in the church and in Christ Jesus
throughout all generations, for ever and ever! Amen.

EPHESIANS 3:20-21

*H*ave you ever dared to dream so big that what you dreamed of seemed nearly impossible to accomplish? Or have you ever thought about the wildest, most improbable thing you could do to honor God with your life?

Now remember, sister: God can do far more through you than what you're imagining, more than you could ever *begin* to dream up for yourself! The same power that raised Jesus from the dead is at work within each person who follows Him (Ephesians 1:17–20). It's the Holy Spirit working through you (Ephesians 3:16).

You may be wondering, *How do I let the Holy Spirit do His work through me?* I'm glad you asked! Here are a few ways:

1. Be prayerful and in His Word.
2. Tune out all distractions so that you can listen to His voice. (You won't be able to hear what He's telling you to do or where He wants you to be if you aren't listening!)

3. Earnestly strive to obey God's will.

Now think about this: God is able to do immeasurably more than you can ask or imagine. Not just a little bit better than you ask. No, *immeasurably*! What God's able to do is so much better than what you can ask or imagine that you can't even measure it. So sister, get quiet, listen for His voice, and start dreaming today.

Britt

God can do far more through you than you could ever begin to dream up for yourself!

19

Embrace Your Brokenness

"I tell you, her many sins have been forgiven; that's why she
loved much. But the one who is forgiven little, loves little."

LUKE 7:47 csb

*W*hich woman in the Bible do you most identify with? If I'm
being totally honest—which I am because we're friends here,
and that's what friends do—I wish I could say I embody the fierce
leadership of the judge and prophet Deborah. I'd love to say I have
the courage of Queen Esther, the loyalty of Ruth, and the work ethic
of Martha, but that wouldn't be true.

Do you know who I identify with the most? The woman in Luke
who showed up at a dinner party with Jesus and some Pharisees, the
one who smashed an alabaster flask of fragrant oil and washed Jesus'
feet with her tear-soaked hair.

Think about this scenario. It'd be something if it happened today.
But in biblical times, to say this behavior was *wild* would be a complete
understatement.

This would have been culturally unacceptable behavior for a man,
but it was punishable for a woman and definitely unpardonable for a
woman of her reputation. (Luke 7:37 says the woman was known to
have a "sinful" reputation, which was a code word for *scandalous*.) This
unnamed woman knew the risk of what she was doing. She counted

the cost, and she decided it was worth the danger if it meant getting close to Jesus.

The party was full of religious men who knew her reputation. Surrounded by her accusers, she dared to approach Jesus. I imagine her with her head hung low, carrying the most valuable thing that belonged to her, painfully aware of her brokenness as she burst open the alabaster flask of fragrant oil. Overcome by emotion, she knelt before Jesus weeping, wetting His feet with her tears. Then she wiped them with her hair, kissed them repeatedly, and poured perfume on them (Luke 7:38).

How often are we like this unnamed woman? When we know we've made a mistake, we fall at the feet of our Savior, overwhelmed with what we've done, doing what little we can to honor Him with the little we have left. If you and I were sitting in the same room right now, you would see me raise my hand because that's been me so many times.

But that's not where the story ends. The gathering was hosted by a Pharisee named Simon, who was curious about Jesus yet suspicious of Him. When Jesus had arrived earlier that night, Simon didn't greet Him with a customary kiss. He didn't anoint Jesus' head with oil or offer Jesus any water so He could wash His feet. Simon's behavior was an intentional diss in this context—and Jesus called out Simon's disrespect by contrasting his behavior with the sinful woman's selfless act of courage.

When you're at your lowest, when you feel like you're broken beyond repair, Jesus is there to put you back together. It's only when you're intimately aware of your need for forgiveness and choose to embrace your brokenness that you're able to experience the fullness of His love.

Cass

Worth More Than
Many Sparrows

"Are not two sparrows sold for a penny? Yet not one of
them will fall to the ground outside your Father's care. And
even the very hairs of your head are all numbered. So don't
be afraid; you are worth more than many sparrows."
MATTHEW 10:29-31

I've got to be honest: the first time I read today's Scripture verses, I
thought to myself, *Hmm, "You are worth more than many sparrows."
So I'm worth more than . . . birds?* But then I dove deeper into the pas-
sage and uncovered that what Jesus was actually saying is much more
profound than comparing our worth to birds.

What He was saying was that our heavenly Father cares about His
creation, down to the birds in the air. Every animal, every bug, every
leaf, every blade of grass is intricately designed and passionately cared
for by God. He made these precious things, and He never forsakes
them. He even clothes them in beauty and glory.

If something as small as a bug is cared for by God, how could we
think that we—created in His image and likeness—are not cared for
or worthy to God?

God cares for us with intention and detail, down to knowing the very number of hair strands on our heads. We are His beloved children, the ones He values dearly. We are His beloved creation, and a Creator always takes care of His creation.

Sister, never forget: you are worthy, loved, and cared for—more than many, many sparrows.

Britt

Our heavenly Father cares about His creation, down to the birds in the air.

Handle with Care

I take pleasure in weaknesses, insults, hardships,
persecutions, and in difficulties, for the sake of
Christ. For when I am weak, then I am strong.

2 CORINTHIANS 12:10 csb

I'm going to be vulnerable for a second: my life is literal chaos right now. Somehow we bought a new home and sold our current home within the same week.

Even good things can be overwhelming sometimes, right?

I'm typing these words from my favorite shabby chic (emphasis on *shabby*) navy-blue chair surrounded by bubble wrap and dozens of cardboard boxes after a weekend of taping up everything we own: clothes, books, picture frames, odds and ends. You name it; it's in a box.

As we unloaded boxes into a storage unit, I noticed our five-year-old daughter doodling on a box that had the word *Fragile* scribbled on the side. Sheer panic washed over me. "Be careful, sweetie! Please hand that to Mommy."

I gently took the box of breakables out of her little hands. For the life of me, I couldn't remember what was packed in that small brown box, but I knew it was valuable and needed to be handled with care.

If I'm honest, at that moment I felt a bit fragile too. It had been a long day—actually, it had been a long week, month, and year. I didn't know how much more I could take, as if I were about to break if I weren't handled with care. Maybe you can relate.

Our lives are consumed with people who need us, and it's easy to forget that we have needs too. As much as we care for others, sometimes we don't remember that we need the same gentle and compassionate care ourselves.

Perhaps you're in the thick of a difficult season, or maybe you're like me and you're overwhelmed by all the good things God has given you to steward. Whatever's making you feel fragile today, I want you to know that God can use this season. Because when we're weak, He's strong. In the moments when you can't push anymore, that's when His almighty strength takes over and you can rest gently in your Father's arms.

No matter what you're up against today, remember this: you are treasured by God. You're worthy of being handled with care. And your fragility is an opportunity for His all-surpassing power to be seen.

Cass

22

Growing Deep Roots

Rooted and built up in him and established in the faith,
just as you were taught, abounding in thanksgiving.

COLOSSIANS 2:7 ESV

The other day I was walking up to my front door, looked down at our landscaping, and saw something growing next to our overgrown hydrangea bush. I bent down for a closer look, and to my surprise, it was actually a tree! I have no idea what kind of tree it was. All I know is that if I were to leave it alone for a few years, it would grow into a full-blown tree just a couple feet from our front door.

Obviously, we couldn't let this tree remain, so I asked my husband, Ryan, to remove it. He didn't think anything of it; he just walked right up to it, grabbed it with both hands, and yanked it out of the soil. It looked effortless. Why? Because the tree didn't have deep roots. Removing it was so easy, barely more difficult than a weed.

Contrast that with the well-established tree in our front yard that has roots so deep, it's messed up our walkway six feet away. The roots of this tree went deep and wide. Trust me, there was no yanking this tree out of the ground. This tree has weathered many storms and will continue to stand firm in the face of many more. The roots are deep enough to move concrete.

So it is with our faith.

If we are firmly planted and have deep roots, God said, "They will be like a tree planted by the water that sends out its roots by the stream. It does not fear when heat comes; its leaves are always green" (Jeremiah 17:8).

In order to stay grounded in our faith, we must be rooted in what God says about us, what He has done through Christ, and our mission while we are here. Then we'll be able to stand firm and weather any storm that is thrown at us, with our roots intact and untouched.

Britt

In order to stay grounded in our faith, we must be rooted in what God says about us.

daily goal:
DESIRE (GOD) MORE
THAN MY NEED FOR
AFFIRMATION AND
VALIDATION FROM
OTHERS.

23

Affirmation Addiction

*Am I now trying to win the approval of human beings, or of
God? Or am I trying to please people? If I were still trying
to please people, I would not be a servant of Christ.*

GALATIANS 1:10

ecause of influencer culture and chasing social media likes,
I'm convinced that our generation is addicted to affirmation.

Here's the deal, friend: we all want to be affirmed. We all want
to know that our friends, colleagues, and loved ones value who we
are and what we contribute to the world. But when our desire to be
validated becomes an obsession, we have a problem.

You might be wondering, *How do I know if I'm addicted to affirmation?* Here's how you know, I think: if every statement you make
about yourself ends in a question, you might be an affirmation addict.
Do you find yourself thinking things like, *Am I enough? Am I loved?
I'm important, right? I'm valued, right?* Time to take a second and think
about why you're so unsure and about the people you want to give you
those kinds of affirmations.

Here's another clue: if you feel like you wouldn't know who you
are if someone doesn't accept you, then you might be an affirmation
addict.

When we begin to seek the validation from other people that

only God can provide, we're treading on dangerous ground. When we determine our value based on the shifting approval of others, and their standards begin to shift, ours will too—not good. And when our worth and identity are built on a shaky foundation, that's where the Enemy can do some of his most effective work.

So take a second to think about where you're finding your worth and whose affirmation you're seeking today. In Galatians 1:10, Paul gave us some great questions to ask ourselves: "Am I now trying to win the approval of human beings, or of God? Or am I trying to please people? If I were still trying to please people, I would not be a servant of Christ."

Sister, today's a good day to break free from affirmation addiction. Make sure you're finding yours in Him.

Cass

When our desire to be validated becomes an obsession, we have a problem.

24

Are Your Problems Bigger Than God?

"Truly I tell you, if you have faith as small as a mustard seed,
you can say to this mountain, 'Move from here to there,'
and it will move. Nothing will be impossible for you."

MATTHEW 17:20

*S*everal years ago my husband and I were traveling quite a bit for work. On our flights I loved to gaze out of the window to see what the world looked like from my viewpoint. Everything looked so tiny. A car was the size of an ant, roads looked like pieces of thread, and lights looked like small specks of glitter sparkling on the ground. Yet sitting right there in the airplane, my soda can appeared larger than everything I was seeing outside the window because of my proximity and perspective.

Since I was physically closer to my soda, it appeared larger than a semitruck thousands of feet below me. Obviously I know a soda can is much smaller than a semi, but in that moment, my eyes told a different story because of the distance between me and my soda versus the ground thousands of feet below.

Similarly, when we become so fixated on our problems, they can seem bigger than anything else. It's as though we have tunnel vision and can't see anything other than what's directly in front of our faces. But what would it look like to change our viewpoint and be so close to God that He's larger and greater than anything else in our lives?

Let's take a quick time-out. Instead of focusing on the problem for a second, let's pull ourselves back to see the size difference between our problems and our God.

Ask yourself this question:

Has my God solved bigger problems than this before?

Of course He has!

Then say this to yourself:

And since that's the case, I know He can help me too.

When you face problems in your life that seem so big, it's time to go to Him. Keep trusting Him, stay close to Him, and He will see you through it.

Britt

Has my God solved bigger problems than this before?

you are
worthy
of the love
and tender
care you
offer others

Friendship Is Worth the Risk

A friend loves at all times, and a brother
is born for a time of adversity.

PROVERBS 17:17

I have a confession: I used to skid through life with surface-level friendships. I know, I know—seems weird for a girl who coleads a ministry, right? But after years of therapy, here's what I've learned about myself: I battle a deep-seated fear that if I ever allowed someone to truly know me, they'd realize I wasn't worthy of their love and leave me.

This fear of abandonment has plagued me most of my life. Even my dearest friends didn't have full access to my heart. I was careful to keep myself at a safe distance. Always willing to listen, but hesitant to share. Quick to offer solidarity, but rarely allowing others to support me. I worried that if I was too heavy, they'd drop me.

If this resonates with you today, I want you to know that you're worthy of the love and tender care you offer others. You can be fully known and fully loved. Yes, guard your heart with wisdom (Proverbs 4:23), but don't wrap it in barbed wire, inflicting pain on anyone who dares to get close. God created us to live in relationship with Him *and* with each other.

My surface-level friendships are a thing of the past, and I'm incredibly grateful for the people God has placed in my life. I have a small circle of close friends who I do life with. We drop off groceries on each other's porches when we know someone is home with a sick child or spouse. We've driven across state lines late into the night and slept in a Walmart parking lot together in a mad dash to show up for a friend who was in desperate need of support and intervention. We've decluttered and packed up each other's homes. We've committed to setting alarms on our phones and taking turns checking in on each other through deployments, grief, and moments of crisis.

These women have taught me what it means to love without restraint. Through their friendship I've learned how to give and receive compassionate care.

If you're afraid of letting people in, you're not alone. I get it. It's risky to let your walls down. When you allow others to get close enough to truly see you, you give them the opportunity to harm you, but you also give them the ability to truly know and love you. A true friend loves at all times, and sisterhood is forged through adversity. God knows we need people to link arms with through hard times and good ones too.

So take the leap: reach out to someone new at church or work for a coffee, or send a text to an old friend. The gesture doesn't have to be huge. You don't have to be best friends immediately. Just spend some time getting to know a friend, and allow yourself to be known. The rewards of true friendship are worth it, I promise.

Cass

26

The Enemy Wants You to Agree with Him. Don't.

Those who live according to the flesh set their minds on the
things of the flesh, but those who live according to the Spirit set
their minds on the things of the Spirit. For to set the mind on the
flesh is death, but to set the mind on the Spirit is life and peace.

ROMANS 8:5-6 ESV

In a court of law, there are usually two sides: the prosecution and the defense. The prosecutor's job is to make a case against the defendant, attempting to convince the judge or jury that the defendant is guilty of harming the plaintiff in some way. The defense attorney's job is to defend the accused client, hoping to show reasonable doubt and attempting to convince the judge or jury that the defendant is innocent.

The Greek word *diabolos*, commonly translated "devil," can also mean "false accuser" or "slanderer."[2] The Enemy loves to speak lies and attempts to get us to think the way he does. A modern courtroom has some aspects of the spiritual battle, especially the battle that takes place in our minds. The devil is the prosecutor, and our Lord Jesus is our defender. Each makes a case. One says you are condemned, a sinner, and gone astray. The other speaks life, grace, and peace.

Here is the thing: in many ways, the Enemy is right. We are sinners, and we have gone astray. We can agree with him that we are deserving of our punishment. But, and this is a huge *but*, Jesus (our defender) already decided to take our place and receive the punishment for our crimes. So, this means that the price has been paid. If the debt has been paid, it's as though the crime no longer exists. It's over—a done deal.

I wish that were the end of it, yet the Enemy doesn't let us off the hook so easily. He knows that he has been defeated, but he doesn't want us to walk in freedom. He reminds us of our past, our mistakes, and says, "This is who you are." He says we are not free.

So the question is: what will you believe about yourself? Will you see yourself as washed clean and free? Or condemned and gone astray? Will we agree with the Enemy or our Lord Jesus? Remember this the next time the Enemy tempts you to think his way.

It could be a simple thought such as believing that you are worthless. If you choose to agree with the Enemy, it will have a detrimental outcome. You will not lift your head high. Your confidence will be destroyed. You will not walk in your full potential in Christ.

What we think matters. Choose today to think the way Jesus wants you to think. You are free. The debt has been paid.

Britt

27

You Are Seen and Known

She gave this name to the Lord who spoke to her:
"You are the God who sees me," for she said, "I
have now seen the One who sees me."

GENESIS 16:13

The Bible teaches us that there's nothing hidden from God (Hebrews 4:13), and yet there have been plenty of moments in my life when I've wondered if God sees me. But there's a story in the Bible that reminds us that no matter the difficulties we face, we are in fact seen and known by God.

Hagar was a pawn in her master's attempt to fulfill a divine promise on their own terms. An enslaved Egyptian woman, Hagar worked in service to Abram and Sarai, who would later be known as Abraham and Sarah. God had come to Abram and told him that he'd be the father of many nations. But Sarai, his wife, still hadn't conceived any children. So Sarai decided to take matters into her own hands and decided to use Hagar to "build" their promised family through her. Forced to be with a man against her will and then found pregnant, Hagar began to despise her mistress, and Sarai began to mistreat her. So Hagar did what any of us would do if we could in that situation: she fled.

Hagar ran as far as her feet could carry her. I can't imagine how lost she must've felt as she wandered deep into the heat of the desert. Thirsty and alone in the wilderness, she encountered God at a well.

In that moment, He called Hagar by name and instructed her to return to the people who oppressed her, but He also offered her a promise: "I will increase your descendants so much that they will be too numerous to count" (Genesis 16:10). Hagar named the Lord *El Roi*, which in Hebrew means "the God who sees me" (Genesis 16:13). She was the first person in the Bible to give God a name—an enslaved woman, an abused runaway. Yet He knew her by name, and she gave Him one too.

What a beautiful reminder that no matter how lost we are, God has never lost sight of us.

The idea that you're seen and known by God might be difficult to wrap your head around. But even when the Enemy tries to convince you that God's gaze has drifted away from you, cling to this truth: He is El Roi, the God who sees you.

Cass

You Are Not Hard to Love

God, being rich in mercy, because of the great love with which
he loved us, even when we were dead in our trespasses, made
us alive together with Christ—by grace you have been saved.

EPHESIANS 2:4-5 ESV

I've believed this lie for many years: *You are too hard to love.*
And here are a few more lies I've held on to: *You're not enough.
You're too much. And you're way too broken for people to love.*

I'm not sure when these lies began to take root, but I find myself
fighting them constantly. Maybe at some point I didn't feel important
to someone who was important to me. Or maybe someone I loved dis-
missed my attempts to seek love and acceptance. No matter how these
began, they have led me to believe that I'm too much for people to love,
which has caused me to try and get love through pleasing other people.
And by now, we all know people-pleasing is an endless quest that'll
never fill the hole in our hearts the way we so desperately want it to.

After years of fighting, I've learned how to combat the lies that tell
me I can't be loved: I replace them with God's truth every single day.

And His truth says:

You are not too hard to love.

Those who didn't love you the way they should have were probably
broken in their own ways, struggling with the same need for love.

You are not too much for Jesus. He sees every part of you and hasn't changed His mind about loving you. Nothing can separate you from His love.

Britt

People-pleasing is an endless quest that'll never fill the hole in our hearts.

GOD CAN
PRODUCE
SWEET FRUIT
OUT OF A
SOUR SEASON

Sweet Fruit Through Sour Seasons

The fruit of the Spirit is love, joy, peace, patience,
kindness, goodness, faithfulness, gentleness, and self-
control. The law is not against such things.
GALATIANS 5:22-23 csb

t feels like life has been an uphill battle lately. And if I'm not careful, the difficulty around me can infiltrate my heart and produce
sin within me. This may look like snapping at my kids when I'm
stressed or wallowing in self-pity instead of keeping my eyes and arms
open to helping someone else. It's tempting to become bitter through
difficult seasons. But here's something I've discovered: if I fix my eyes
on God when I'm in a hard season, He can still produce good fruit
within me, even when everything around me is sour.

When I'm frustrated or overwhelmed, one of the things I do to
calm my heart and adjust my attitude is something pretty simple: I
proclaim the fruit of the Spirit (Galatians 5:22–23) out loud. It might
sound weird, but I promise it works. So try it with me! Take a second and say each of these words out loud. It may sound goofy, but I
promise it'll make you feel better: love, joy, peace, patience, kindness,
goodness, faithfulness, gentleness, and self-control.

What do you think? How do you feel now?

Saying these verses aloud doesn't make all my problems go away, but it *does* reorient my heart toward God and away from fixating on all the things I'm struggling with. Even in your sour seasons, God can still produce good, sweet fruit in you.

Here's a random question (that's not so random, I promise): are you familiar with how wine was made during biblical times? People stomped barefoot on grapes, then the juice collected was placed in earthen vats and stored in a cool, dark place to begin fermentation. What if the pressure we're experiencing is squeezing rich new wine out of us?

Let's dig our roots deep into the Word of God and abide in Him. He is our Vine (John 15:1), and through Him, we can experience the production of sweet fruit regardless of the sour seasons we walk through.

Cass

30

The Real You

I praise you because I am fearfully and wonderfully made.

PSALM 139:14

*I*n order to grasp, understand, and walk in the power of who you *are*, you must first make peace with who you *aren't*.

This is who you aren't:

Your failures
Your past mistakes
Your Pinterest-perfect home
Your greatest wins
Your success
Your appearance
Your social media likes
Your relationship status
Your size
Your flaws
Your roles
Your responsibilities
Your job
Your social media following
Your trauma
Your qualifications
Your income

Your status in society

Your rejection

Your abandonment

This is who you are, in Christ. (As you read, declare each one out loud!)

You are fearfully and wonderfully made (Psalm 139:14).

You are God's masterpiece (Ephesians 2:10).

You are made in His image (Genesis 1:27).

You are forgiven (1 John 1:9).

You are redeemed by God (Ephesians 1:7–8).

You are called by name, not by your sin (Isaiah 43:1).

You are a new creation—the old life is gone (2 Corinthians 5:17).

You are greatly loved by God (Romans 8:31–39).

You are His child (1 John 3:1).

You are an heir of God and coheir with Christ (Romans 8:17).

You are a member of God's family (Ephesians 2:19).

You are blessed (Ephesians 1:3).

You are chosen to be part of a royal priesthood, a holy nation set apart for God (1 Peter 2:9).

You are His treasured possession (Deuteronomy 14:2).

You are precious to God (Isaiah 43:4).

This is what God says about you. Look at this list often. Say it out loud. Declare it over your life. Let it sink in. Measure your thoughts against these truths. If your thoughts don't line up, trash them and replace them with the truth above.

Britt

31

The Light You Carry

What we preach is not ourselves, but Jesus Christ as
Lord, and ourselves as your servants for Jesus' sake. For
God, who said, "Let light shine out of darkness," made
his light shine in our hearts to give us the light of the
knowledge of God's glory displayed in the face of Christ.

2 CORINTHIANS 4:5-6

I didn't grow up in a religious home, and my brother once jokingly referred to me as "the white sheep of the family." In some circles, this might be taken as a compliment. But in my case, I knew it was intended as a not-so-subtle jab at me and Christianity.

Although I've had the incredible privilege of seeing my family come to the soul-anchoring decision to follow Jesus, there were some challenging years leading up to it. We had plenty of awkward conversations and ugly confrontations. At one point I was even accused of joining a cult because I was at church whenever the doors were open and, in my family members' words, "That just ain't normal." Ha ha! We can laugh about it now, but at the time it was difficult to imagine that anything would ever change.

Admittedly, in that season I was pretty immature in my faith. I often lacked humility in situations in which I could have offered my family more nuance and empathy. Have you ever been there too?

If you have people in your life who aren't believers, can I offer some advice? The life you live and the choices you make are more effective for sharing the gospel than any sermon you could ever preach. The light you carry as you live in love will look much different from the people around you.

Now, sometimes the light you carry will irritate the people in your life if they've been sitting in the dark, kind of like turning on a bright light in a dark room. But don't be discouraged. It isn't always you. Often it's the conviction of the Holy Spirit, who dwells within you. And as they did with my family, over time the kindness and love they experience may lead them to repentance (Romans 2:4).

So don't forget: the light you carry will speak for itself because your actions speak louder than your words. The people in your life need to see you practicing what you preach. Lead with love, and allow His light to shine through you, pointing people to the hope we have in Him.

Cass

32

God Is the Ultimate Comfort Provider

God is our refuge and strength, an ever-present help in trouble.
PSALM 46:1

What do you turn to when you're in need of comfort?

When my eyes aren't fixed on Jesus, I turn to things like TV, food, social media, gossip, shopping, and spending money. These activities don't actually comfort me—not really. They just distract me from the painful situation I want to avoid.

Here's the thing: none of us likes to be uncomfortable or stressed. It makes sense why we allow ourselves to become distracted so easily. It's a lot easier to reach for a bag of chips or turn on our favorite show than it is to face the difficult situation that requires us to rise to the occasion and fix it or, if we can't fix it, to sit with the discomfort.

The hard truth is, when we try to fill our attention with distractions, we're not allowing ourselves to truly heal from our pain. In fact, the Enemy exploits our need for comfort by pulling us away from the ultimate Comforter, Jesus, and he tries to make sure we stay away from sitting at His feet when we're in need of healing.

But don't forget, friend: when we allow ourselves to turn to anything other than Christ for comfort, we're just prolonging our own suffering.

The Bible says we are to cast our cares and burdens upon Him because He cares for us (1 Peter 5:7). So even if we're tempted to distract ourselves from our pain, let's step out of our comfort zone. Let's be willing to be uncomfortable. Let's turn to Him to provide us with comfort, care, and healing so we can continue doing good work for Him.

Britt

When we try to fill our attention with distractions, we're not allowing ourselves to truly heal from our pain.

33

Cultivate Deep Friendships

Draw near to God, and he will draw near to you.

JAMES 4:8 CSB

*H*ere's something you don't hear every day: my husband and I have spent the majority of our marriage living in a different state from our closest friends and family. Crazy, right? As a former military spouse, I've become all too familiar with the experience of saying goodbye. This means that up until recently, I've spent my adult life being resistant to planting my roots down too deeply.

But since my husband accepted a civilian position with the US Department of Defense, we've found ourselves in uncharted territory, remaining in one place for longer than anywhere else our family has ever lived.

When my husband was in the military, I became comfortable with living as a nomad. Navigating one major life transition after another without a strong support network was hard, of course, but nothing could've prepared me for the difficulty of finding and establishing meaningful community. Honestly, I found it easier to fend off feelings of loneliness when I thought we were somewhere for a short season. But being stationary intensified my feelings of isolation, and for the first time in a *really* long time, I had been aching to be part of a community. Add in a global pandemic and working from home, and I was bound to feel disconnected eventually.

It can be difficult to make new friends, find a new church home, and integrate into a supportive local community. It can feel awkward to put yourself out there, to ask someone new to go for coffee when you don't know the first thing about her. Sometimes it feels like going on another first date (and we all know how fun those are).

But sister, a strong, supportive community is worth fighting for. God made us to do life together. And as hard as it is to cultivate community, to intentionally ask someone how she's doing when you're in the middle of your mess, to show up for someone and watch her kids while she's in the middle of *her* mess—I promise, it's worth it.

After being stationary instead of being stationed somewhere else, I now have those friends who "stick closer than a brother" (or sister!) that Proverbs 18:24 talks about. I cherish those relationships. I love every time I get a "How's your heart?" text from a trusted friend. I love knowing that I can pour my heart out to the women closest to me and receive encouragement, wisdom, and so much love in return.

It takes intentional work to cultivate community right where you are. And as you till the soil, remember that even in your lonely moments, God is always right by your side. His Word promises that if you draw near to Him, He will draw near to you (James 4:8). So take heart, sister. As you build the community you long for, you're never, ever alone.

Cass

THE CROSS OF *Christ* DEFINES YOUR TRUE WORTH

34

The Freedom Framework

"You belong to your father, the devil, and you want to carry out your father's desires. He was a murderer from the beginning, not holding to the truth, for there is no truth in him. When he lies, he speaks his native language, for he is a liar and the father of lies."

JOHN 8:44

In Scripture, Jesus described Satan as the "father of lies" (John 8:44). And as you can see in today's verse, it says that when the Enemy lies, "he speaks his native language."

Here's something I've noticed about the Enemy's lies: they're often the direct opposite of what God says. There is absolutely no truth in Satan. Jesus is the way, the *truth*, and the life.

Here's something else I've noticed: lies aren't just things that are spoken to us. Lies are also false beliefs we allow to fester in our hearts that can destroy our peace and leave us wounded.

You could believe a lie your entire life and function out of a deeply wounded place and not realize it until you compare the lie to the truth. Let's break it down:

Lie: *I'm less loved or worthy with more fat on my body.*
How I act on the lie: *I starve and abuse my body.*
How it affects my life: *I hide from people because I hate how I look.*

The wound it leaves: *I hate the body that God gave me.*

Truth: *I'm who God made me to be* (Psalm 139:13–14).

How I act on the truth: *I take care of my body and glorify God with it* (1 Corinthians 6:19–20).

How the truth affects my life: *I am free from the weight of the expectations of others and the number on the scale. My true worth is hidden in Christ* (Colossians 3:3).

The healing I receive: *I love my body, and I'm thankful for it every day.*

The next time you begin to feel bad about yourself, stop and think for a second. Are you believing the father of lies? Or do you need to remember what your heavenly Father, the Father of truth, is telling you? Break it down, and you'll see His truth.

Britt

35

God's Not Mad at You

Where can I go from your Spirit? Where can I flee from your
presence? If I go up to the heavens, you are there; if I make
my bed in the depths, you are there. If I rise on the wings of
the dawn, if I settle on the far side of the sea, even there your
hand will guide me, your right hand will hold me fast. If I say,
"Surely the darkness will hide me and the light become night
around me," even the darkness will not be dark to you; the
night will shine like the day, for darkness is as light to you.

PSALM 139:7–12

There was a season in my life when I was actively avoiding God. I
wish I could say I'm being dramatic, but it's true.

I was twenty-one years old, and I had watched just about every
part of my life shatter before my eyes. I was fired from what I thought
was my dream job. I lost my apartment and was couch surfing without
a place to call home. And on top of it all, my self-worth crumbled as I
endured the devastating end of a toxic four-year relationship.

Just thinking about this season makes me wince. It lasted only a
few weeks, but the repercussions of wandering far from God affected
me for years.

I was lonely, confused, and angry at God. I was hurting and looking for my worth in all the wrong places. I was numbing the pain of

loneliness with male attention and affection. I wrongly thought that my body and appearance were the most valuable things I had to offer. It hurts to share that, but it was true of twenty-one-year-old Cass. I was miserable and desperate to numb the pain I was walking through. I avoided church, and I tried to ignore the conviction of the Holy Spirit. It wasn't until I found myself at an all-time low that I realized that no matter how lost I felt, God never lost sight of me.

If you're angry and you've wandered away from God, I want to encourage you with this truth: God's not mad at you. Actually, He loves you so, so much. And there's nothing you can do that will separate you from His love (Romans 8:38–39). No matter how far you've wandered away from God, you'll never escape His sight—or His love.

Cass

No matter how lost I felt, God never lost sight of me.

36

Weight May Fluctuate, but Worth Does Not

God said, "Let us make man in our image, after our likeness. And let them have dominion over the fish of the sea and over the birds of the heavens and over the livestock and over all the earth and over every creeping thing that creeps on the earth."

GENESIS 1:26 ESV

I'd be a rich gal if I had a dollar for every time my weight has fluctuated throughout my life. I'm not the type of person who can pig out and not see a difference on the scale. I wish I were, though, because I could snack on chips like it's my job.

Stress, pregnancy, marriage—they've all been factors in my tendency to overeat and gain. Have you ever heard of the term "happy weight"? One year into marriage, and I had put on a whopping thirty "happy" pounds.

Let me tell you something: I was underweight when my husband and I got married because I struggled with anorexia. I've since found freedom from my eating disorder, but when I was at my thinnest, I thought I had "arrived." In reality, I didn't feel content the way I thought I would when I finally reached my goal weight. I still looked in the mirror and saw a fat person.

The cat-and-mouse chase of a skinnier me interfered with my ability to see the truth that my worth was never meant to rise and fall based on the number on the scale. It's always been, and always will be, safely and securely hidden in Christ.

The problem with finding my value and worth as a woman in my size is that my size will always fluctuate. Just when I think I've arrived again, "Miss Flo" makes her monthly appearance or I go to a birthday party and have some cake, or whatever the case may be. I'm so exhausted from chasing a moving target.

Friend, you deserve to break free from the shackles of your weight determining your worth. The measure of your waist is not synonymous with the measure of your worth. Do what you can to end the chase, and know that your worth in Christ always remains the same. No matter what size you may be or what the scale reads, your worth in Christ never fluctuates.

Britt

37

When Growing Feels Like Breaking

"He cuts off every branch in me that bears no fruit, while every branch that does bear fruit he prunes so that it will be even more fruitful."

JOHN 15:2

*H*ave you ever planted a summer garden? It can be so gratifying to watch all the vegetables and flowers grow from small seedlings into big, beautiful plants. Humans are kind of like that too. It's fun to watch people you know and love flourish into a new chapter of their lives. But here's the thing about growth that nobody talks about: at first, it can feel like you're breaking apart.

But think about planting a seed. In order to sprout, a seed needs to spend some time underneath the soil, in a dark and unseen place. And then it has to break open for the roots to begin to take hold of the soil, which will give the seed—and the plant it will eventually become—a strong foundation.

Going through a season of growing can feel scary, especially when you can't see the way forward. When change or things you've never experienced before begin to happen, it can feel overwhelming to try to figure out your new normal. But don't forget the old saying: if

God brings you *to* it, He'll bring you *through* it. And sister, what He's bringing you through will help you flourish in the beautiful life He's planted you in.

So if you're going through a season of growing pains, please know that God is *not* going to let you break. He is in the soil just as much as in the growth. If the soil is good, the growth will come.

This is something I pray in my own seasons of growth. I hope it helps you too.

Gracious and heavenly Father, if this ache is what it takes for growth to break through, then bring on the breaking. Help me take root in Your firm foundation, and help me flourish into the story You're writing just for me. I trust You to grow something new and wonderful in my life. In all the change I'm going through, please help me lean on You. In the mighty name of Jesus I pray, amen.

Cass

FEAR IS A LIAR

Fear Is Lying to You

There is no fear in love. But perfect love drives out
fear, because fear has to do with punishment. The
one who fears is not made perfect in love.

1 JOHN 4:18

*W*e all fear bad news. When everything is smooth sailing, we all fear the rug being ripped out from under us.

Let's face it: sometimes our minds are more hardwired for anticipating the worst-case scenarios than for trusting God to work in all situations for our good.

As I was rocking my daughter to sleep one night, I found myself caught up in the immense fear that something bad might happen to her. The fear I felt was suffocating me, choking the breath out of my lungs as I fixated on what could go wrong.

In that moment of gripping fear, the heavenly Father gently spoke to me: "The rug can't be ripped out from under you when you stand on Me, daughter."

Oh, how that pierced my heart. I imagined being a little girl afraid to dance, so I stood on my Father's feet as He moved me around the dance floor. I was able to shift my focus from "What could go wrong?" to "Be thankful for what God has done and what He's going to do."

There's something about cultivating thankfulness that tends to silence fear, anxiety, and worry. Thankfulness helps us to pull our fixation off the worst-case scenarios and put it on what God has already done.

Remember, fear has to do with punishment. The Enemy wants us to believe that our destiny is punishment rather than salvation by grace.

But fear is lying to you, friend. Unsubscribe from the false narrative that God has somehow abandoned you or will abandon you. On the days when you're fearing the worst, choose to focus on the fact that you are in Christ. You stand on Him: the firm foundation. Christ in you, the hope of glory. Fear can't break you because the One who holds you together is perfect, and His love keeps you secure.

Fear has no place here, in Jesus' name.

Britt

"The rug can't be ripped out from under you when you stand on Me, daughter."

39

A Love That Tears Down Walls

*If, then, there is any encouragement in Christ, if any consolation
of love, if any fellowship with the Spirit, if any affection and
mercy, make my joy complete by thinking the same way, having
the same love, united in spirit, intent on one purpose. Do nothing
out of selfish ambition or conceit, but in humility consider others
as more important than yourselves. Everyone should look not
to his own interests, but rather to the interests of others.*

PHILIPPIANS 2:1-4 csb

Listen, I get it. The internet is loud. It seems like there's a constant demand for us to take a stand on the issue of the day, to pick a side and stay there. But what if there's a different way? What if we could lead with humility and still stand firm in our faith?

I know this isn't a popular line of thought, but hang with me for a moment. The Enemy tries hard to convince us that we have to tear down the people we don't agree with, but you know what God says? He wants us to love other people, no matter which side they're on (Luke 6:35). I know it's hard, but I believe it's possible for us to stand our ground without trampling on other people. And guess what? Those are the very people God has called us to consider as more important than ourselves (Philippians 2:3–4).

Dear friend, right now we're living within the tension of Christian humility, and it's downright messy. The world will push us to the right and pull us to the left. But in Christ, only one direction honors all people in God's sight, and that is upward. It's only when we're able to fix our eyes above, directly on Him, that we're able to see others clearly.

You already know this, but let me remind you: it's so important that we treat all people with God-given dignity, regardless of their opinions on policy and politics. There is no partiality in Christ and no assigned seating in heaven. And through the cross, we can find common ground. In Philippians 2:1 (CSB), the word *fellowship* comes from the Greek word *koinonia*, which means "the sharing of things in common."[3] Through the power of the Holy Spirit, we're able to participate in sacred communion with believers who've lived vastly different experiences than we have and hold perspectives we may never have considered.

Here's what I'm not saying: "To love our enemies is to never disagree." Here's what I *am* saying: "We can honor God and love those whom we disagree with." The world will know that we belong to Christ because of the way we love each other (John 13:35). So let's be a people who genuinely look after the interests of others and live with uncommon humility. You know what that does? It enables us to offer mercy to each other in a world that so desperately needs it. It allows us to forge relationships with the type of unity that escapes explanation outside of Jesus.

Living within the tension of Christian humility isn't easy. It isn't always comfortable. But love is messy, love is costly, and God is worthy of everything we have to give. Let's lay down our pride and live lives worthy of His sacrifice.

Cass

40

Reflecting God's Image

We are ambassadors for Christ, God making his appeal through
us. We implore you on behalf of Christ, be reconciled to God.

2 CORINTHIANS 5:20 ESV

When our daughter, Ariana, was ten months old, she was exploring her newfound skill: walking. Well, her version of walking at that time was pretty wobbly, but she was enjoying herself. She would walk past our mirror, see her image in the reflection, and think it was another baby playing peek-a-boo. It was super cute.

Scripture says we were made in God's image (Genesis 1:27), and that when we accept Christ as our Lord and Savior, we become "ambassadors for Christ" (2 Corinthians 5:20 ESV). An ambassador is a representative who speaks for another, usually someone royal or with executive power. In this scenario, we get to represent our King, and we're called to spread the good news in a place that is not our home.

Representing Christ is a pretty big deal, not one to take lightly. So how do we take on that responsibility and do it well?

In John 14:12, Jesus said, "Whoever believes in me will also do the works that I do" (ESV). And as His ambassador, we are empowered to act as He would. The fruit of the Spirit is love, joy, peace, patience, kindness, goodness, faithfulness, gentleness, and self-control

(Galatians 5:22–23). Every time we display these characteristics, we are rightly representing our King.

So the next time you walk past a mirror, remember that you are called to reflect God's image to the world—a world that desperately needs Him.

Britt

Representing Christ is a pretty big deal, not one to take lightly.

41

Wisdom, the Ultimate Hidden Treasure

How much better to get wisdom than gold,
to get insight rather than silver!
PROVERBS 16:16

I was recently having my quiet time with the Lord—surrounded by three rowdy, tiny humans, I suppose you could call it my not-so-quiet time—when my oldest daughter asked me why I'm always reading my Bible. I jokingly responded, "Because a proverb a day keeps the foolishness away!" She stared at me puzzled, clearly not grasping the lame joke I tried to make. So I leaned in and explained to her what I meant.

If we want to live a life that is guided by God, we have to seek God's wisdom every day by reading His Word. The book of Proverbs is a great place to integrate bite-size truth into our daily lives. There are thirty-one chapters in the book of Proverbs, which means we can read literally one chapter a day, every single month. Proverbs 16:16 tells us that pursuing biblical wisdom is far more valuable than any fortune we could earn in the world. We can't take earthly riches with us into eternity, but wisdom is a treasure that death cannot separate us from.

To be rich in wisdom is to possess a wealth beyond anything this earthly life can offer. If you're like me, you've learned plenty of life's lessons the hard way. You'll be happy to know that Proverbs 2:4 tells us that if we seek wisdom like we search for hidden treasure, we'll discover the knowledge of God. What a beautiful promise! If we commit ourselves to seeking insight and understanding from the Word of God, we're guaranteed to find the wisdom we're looking for.

Cass

If we want to live a life that is guided by God, we have to seek God's wisdom every day by reading His Word.

TO BE VULNERABLE
IS TO surrender

42

Getting Real with God

Cast all your anxiety on him because he cares for you.

1 PETER 5:7

I've heard more about vulnerability in the last decade than I have in a lifetime.

I think that's because we're seeing how important it is for your soul to align with what you say and do. It's important to share your convictions and be your real self with others. That's how integrity is born.

But I've got to be honest: it's hard to be vulnerable because being vulnerable means putting yourself at risk of being hurt or rejected. But there is so much beauty in being "real" with the people in your life, and that especially includes God.

I know it can feel scary to get real with God, especially when you don't feel like you're worthy to be in His presence. But you can trust Him, I promise. Here are a few reasons why:

1. He will never leave you or abandon you (Isaiah 49:15–16).
2. He keeps His promises (1 Kings 8:56).
3. He doesn't change (Hebrews 13:8).
4. Nothing can separate you from His love (Romans 8:38–39).

You're safe with God, sister. And when you draw near to Him, here's the good part: you don't have to deal with your pain alone. He invites you to cast your burdens on Him because He cares for you.

So get real with Him. Be transparent about your struggles. He sees you, He knows you, and He loves you just as you are. And remember: to be vulnerable is to surrender. So surrender your heart to Him, and you'll receive His healing, comfort, and peace.

Britt

You can Trust Him, I promise.

43

Just in the Nick of Time

Abraham looked up and saw a ram caught in the thicket by
its horns. So Abraham went and took the ram and offered
it as a burnt offering in place of his son. And Abraham
named that place The LORD Will Provide, so today it is
said, "It will be provided on the LORD's mountain."

GENESIS 22:13-14 CSB

*H*ave you ever been in a difficult situation and desperately needed God to provide on your behalf? I sure have—many, many times.

As I mentioned earlier, at twenty-one I lost what I thought was my dream job. I endured the brutal end of a toxic, four-year relationship with a guy I thought I was going to marry. And as if matters weren't dire enough, rent was due for my apartment, and I couldn't pay it. To me, it seemed like I was living in a poorly written country song. Everything was going wrong, and I couldn't see an end in sight.

I was breaking down daily, and I'm not talking about my beat-up '97 Honda Accord. My life was a mess, and I needed God's provision desperately. With little resources, limited support, and a new full-time job, I decided to enroll myself in the local community college. Conveniently there was an opening for a job on campus as the resident assistant of the women's dorm. With nowhere to live and nothing left to lose, I applied, got the position, and suddenly found myself a place to sleep that didn't require couch surfing. (Thanks, God!)

During that season of life, I felt like I was falling behind my peers, and I was struggling to keep up in every possible way. At twenty-two, I heard a wise mentor describe God as "Jehovah Nick of Time" because He always shows up and provides just in the nick of time. I've carried this phrase close to my heart ever since because I've found it to be true. When God sets your pace, it's covered by His grace, and His provision is always on time.

There's a story in Genesis 22:1–14 that, to me, fully illustrates this "Jehovah Nick of Time" idea. God decided to test Abraham's faith and asked him to sacrifice his son, Isaac, the one Abraham had waited literally decades to hold in his arms. Abraham didn't skip a beat. He immediately responded to God with obedience and took his son to the place where God directed him and placed Isaac on the altar. But just in the nick of time, God came through. He stopped Abraham and showed him a ram in a thicket to sacrifice instead. Abraham responded to God's empathy by naming that place Jehovah-jireh, which means "The Lord Will Provide."

If you're going through a difficult situation and desperately need God to intervene on your behalf, can I encourage you with something? God is present with you in the midst of your struggle. You can trust God with your every need because He is Jehovah-jireh, the God who provides.

Cass

44

If You've Wandered
Away from God,
Read This

"He returned home to his father. And while he was still a long way
off, his father saw him coming. Filled with love and compassion,
he ran to his son, embraced him, and kissed him. His son said
to him, 'Father, I have sinned against both heaven and you, and
I am no longer worthy of being called your son.' But his father
said to the servants, 'Quick! Bring the finest robe in the house
and put it on him. Get a ring for his finger and sandals for his
feet. And kill the calf we have been fattening. We must celebrate
with a feast, for this son of mine was dead and has now returned
to life. He was lost, but now he is found.' So the party began."

LUKE 15:20-24 NLT

You've found yourself wandering, in a place where you swore to
yourself you wouldn't be lost again.

Your aching heart is flooded with sorrow because you aren't sure if
He will still love you. You aren't sure if He'll take you back. You aren't
sure if it's okay to show Him the darkness you've subjected yourself to.
You aren't sure if you'll be forgiven.

You're afraid to come home.

He's seen you. He's watched you wander. He's seen you trying to find your own way in the lost path that leads to emptiness.

All the while, His arms were outstretched.

Not once did He look at you with crossed arms, as if He had changed His mind about you.

His arms are open.

Waiting for you.

Drawing you out of darkness.

Kissing your brokenness with redemption and love.

The truth is, He has never stopped loving you.

You will always be His, and you will always belong to Him.

He has seen your unloveliness, and none of it changed His mind about loving you.

Because *nothing* can separate you from His love.

Sin creates distance.

But His love covers over a multitude of sins.

His love remains the same.

So, friend, come home.

As long as your heart is still beating, His invitation for you never expires.

He is the Father waiting on the porch with the door open calling out your name.

He is the Father running to you to embrace you upon arrival.

Come home.

Crawl into His arms.

And stay with Him.

You are found.

Britt

45

Iron Sharpens Iron

As iron sharpens iron, so one person sharpens another.

PROVERBS 27:17

I like to surround myself with people who challenge me, because I firmly believe that healthy relationships and friendships require a little friction—just enough to spark refinement through honest conversations. I appreciate people who hold differing opinions and values from my own, especially when I'm in close relationship with them.

It might be hard to believe, but by nature I tend to avoid conflict. And I've learned it's dangerous to surround myself with people who like me only when I agree with them. I remember a time when living to obtain approval of every person in my life left me living within the confines of their expectations. And eventually, as I began to find my voice and speak out when I held a different view, those friends began to disengage. At first it was painful to lose people I thought were close to me. But as time went on, I realized that their friendship was surface level and conditional upon my compliance.

Occasionally people have said to me, "You've changed," and to that I respond, "Thank God." I'm grateful I've been able to outgrow places where I wasn't intended to stay. I'm glad I've met people who have different experiences and perspectives, who challenge me and call out the goodness of God within me. I'm thankful I have people in my life who love me enough to engage in difficult conversations and lovingly correct me when I'm wrong. It's a gift to be in fellowship with believers who invite me to consider what it's like to walk a day in their shoes instead of dodging discomfort and denying we've walked different paths.

These types of friendships require friction because they ignite refinement. As Proverbs 27:17 reminds us, "As iron sharpens iron, so one person sharpens another." We have to be willing to feel the discomfort of challenging conversations, driven by conviction and sealed with empathy.

So if you want to grow in wisdom, surround yourself with people who will sharpen you.

Cass

I'm grateful I've been able to outgrow places where I wasn't intended to stay.

46

Die to Self, Live for Purpose

Then he said to them all: "Whoever wants to be my disciple must
deny themselves and take up their cross daily and follow me."

LUKE 9:23

ometimes the Bible has some interesting instructions for us, such
as to die to ourselves, to deny ourselves, to put off the flesh, and
to pick up our cross daily to follow Jesus. Heavy? A little. But what
does that all really mean? Let's take it apart, one by one.

First of all, in order to pick up our cross, we must first lay something
else down.

In Galatians 2:20 the apostle Paul stated, "I have been crucified
with Christ and I no longer live, but Christ lives in me. The life I now
live in the body, I live by faith in the Son of God, who loved me and
gave himself for me."

The call to die to ourselves and put off our flesh implies that the
old self must die in order for the new self to come to life and thrive
(John 3:3–7). When we come to Christ and are born again into a new
life in Him, dying to ourselves is part of the process of sanctification.
It is a daily decision to put aside our own plans and seek to follow His
instead. This isn't just a one-time event, either. It's an ongoing, lifelong
process of living a life with Christ in you.

Now, let's take a look at how to die to ourselves:

1. We give up the right to put ourselves first (Philippians 2:3–4).
2. We deny the desires and pleasures of the world (1 Timothy 6:6–10).
3. We trust in the Lord without leaning on our own understanding (Proverbs 3:5).
4. We walk by the Spirit, not by the flesh (Galatians 5:16).

You might ask: *Is it possible to die to myself and still thrive in a culture that encourages me to put myself first?*

To that, I pose two other questions: What if living a purpose-filled, Christlike life has nothing to do with living within the culturally constructed walls of self-focus and self-consciousness? What if finding who we really are in Christ requires us to lose who we thought we were?

Dying to ourselves doesn't mean that we neglect our souls. It's the opposite, actually. Dying to ourselves focuses our intention on *caring* for our souls. Because when we do, we recognize our deeper need for our Savior. We allow ourselves to hear His call by lowering the volume of our own desires and aligning ourselves with His.

It might feel like you're losing a lot when you deny yourself, but you are gaining so much more in Christ. The cost might seem like a lot up front. But I can assure you that the payoff is well worth it.

Britt

THERE IS *freedom* IN LIVING FROM YOUR WORTH, NOT FOR IT.

47

When Hard Truths Hurt

Speaking the truth in love, we will grow to become in every respect the mature body of him who is the head, that is, Christ.

EPHESIANS 4:15

I didn't go to lunch that day expecting my best friend to hand me a gentle rebuke, but that's exactly what happened. And I'm so grateful she did.

The conversation started out like they always do—catching up on kids, husbands, and all the latest—when we started talking about a relationship I'd been having a problem with for a while. I was giving so much more than the other person was offering to me, and while I was grateful for what this person *could* offer, it just wasn't enough. As I was telling this to my friend across the table, she got quiet—like, *really* quiet. After an awkward pause, I could hear the strain in her voice as she said, "I'm not saying you shouldn't be grateful for the crumbs. Absolutely, be grateful for everything God has given you. But what I am trying to tell you is that you're worthy of more than just the scraps others are willing to give to you."

I'm going to be honest with you: hearing my best friend say this stung a bit. It hurt to hear the truth, even though I know it came from a place of love (Ephesians 4:15). But as I've grown in my faith, I've learned that sometimes spiritual maturity means swallowing hard truths and receiving correction from the trustworthy people in your life.

As much as I didn't want it, as much as I wasn't looking for it, I needed someone to call out the false belief I was clinging to. Subconsciously, I thought I deserved to be treated poorly. And I had allowed my gratitude to become a license for others to sin against me. *Oof.* It was hard for me to comprehend that I was worthy of being treated with dignity. It hurts to even admit that I once believed this to be true.

I'm so grateful God used my dear friend to help me uproot these harmful false beliefs. Relational equity should always determine the authority someone has to speak into our lives. Not every voice we hear is a voice we need to heed, but we do need people who will boldly speak the truth to us in love. We need people who love us enough to correct us when we've clung to a false belief. In an abundance of counselors, there is safety (Proverbs 11:14).

Cass

48

The Girl Who Forgets Who She Is

Do not merely listen to the word, and so deceive yourselves.
Do what it says. Anyone who listens to the word but
does not do what it says is like someone who looks at
his face in a mirror and, after looking at himself, goes
away and immediately forgets what he looks like.

JAMES 1:22-24

I don't know about you, but I can't even remember what I ate for lunch yesterday. I have a terrible memory most of the time, yet I can remember the birthday of someone I've met only once. I guess it just depends on the situation.

Sometimes, even for a quick moment, I forget who I am in Christ. I have interactions in which I respond from my flesh or see myself as worthless when comparison wins my focus.

In those moments of forgetting who I am, the Lord gently whispers to me, "It's okay, daughter. You just forgot who you were for a moment."

It reminds me of today's verses in James that talk about not just reading the Word but doing what it says by applying it. This last phrase is key. When we take in the Word without applying it, it's as though we've looked in the mirror and immediately forgotten what we look like as soon as we walked away.

Let's face it: we need to be reminded by God's Word of who we

THE GIRL WHO FORGETS WHO SHE IS

are. The devil is in the business of trying to distort the truth of what God says of us, even if it's a truth we already know. No matter what, the Enemy seems intent to kill, steal, and destroy.

He wants to kill our relationship with God.

He wants to steal our identity and replace it with a counterfeit.

He wants to destroy our future.

But I've got good news for you: no scheme of his can separate you from the love of God.

He can try, but he will fail.

His future is sealed.

And so is yours, in Christ.

Let's dive into God's Word and stay in it.

Let's keep His Word written on the tablet of our hearts so we don't forget who we are and whose we are.

Britt

Let's face it: we need to be reminded by God's Word of who we are.

49

When You Don't Feel Like Enough, Jesus Is

My God will meet all your needs according to
the riches of his glory in Christ Jesus.
PHILIPPIANS 4:19

*C*an I be vulnerable with you for a second? I spent a good portion of my life feeling inadequate.

For decades I suffered with crippling anxiety, and I found myself overwhelmed by my inability to be "enough." I constantly felt as though I could never measure up. And if I'm being totally honest—which I am because I love you enough to tell you the truth—I was deeply unstable in my relationship with God until I was in my late twenties. I know I'm not alone in struggling in my walk with God or feeling like I'm not enough. But weirdly enough, I think they go hand in hand.

In a world that drives us to constantly do more and be more, even when we try our hardest, we're never going to be perfect. We're never going to measure up to these impossible standards. If we're using the world as our measuring stick, it's no wonder so many of us are tempted to seek validation in all the wrong places.

But you know what? Thankfully, God's love and goodness aren't reliant on our "enoughness." He gives them to us freely and in abundance.

Dear friend, if you're trying so hard to do enough and be enough, remember that His "grace is sufficient for you" (2 Corinthians 12:9). This means you don't have to measure up to anyone or for anyone else. Jesus is enough, so you don't have to be. Today's a good day for your striving to cease. His strength is found in your weakness, and where you lack, He fills in the gap.

So let's do something radical! Let's choose to forfeit the endless pursuit of becoming enough. Instead, let's break free from insecurity and live confident of our true worth and identity found in Jesus. Ready, set, *go*!

Cass

God's love and goodness aren't reliant on our "enoughness."

50

Lost and Louis Vuitton

"Where your treasure is, there your heart will be also."

MATTHEW 6:21

I've always had a love for designer bags. The scent of the pristine leather, the flawless stitching, the gold hardware—the quintessential icons of success in handbag form. Nothing says, "I've made it," quite like having designer things. Or so we're told.

It's easy to get lost in the world of accumulating treasures for ourselves. I've been—and sometimes still am—the person who desires to be viewed as having it all together by having nice things: the best shoes, the best designer bags, a nice car. But at what cost? Usually a pretty high one, actually.

Spending loads of money on material things to be seen as worthy and important is a cheap trade. It's one that requires high investment on your end, but has a low payoff. If you have nice things, it's not inherently wrong. But if you're not okay when you *don't* have those things, then you've got a problem.

God's Word perfectly describes why storing up treasures for ourselves on earth is a total waste. If our identity is attached to the items we own, then what happens when those things are gone?

Don't put all your stock into accumulating things on earth. Invest in the things that truly matter. Instead of that designer handbag, decide to carry love with you. Don't reach for the Louboutins with the ruby-red soles; choose to walk with purpose. Instead of getting behind the wheel of a luxury car, let faith steer you where you need to go.

You'll get a greater yield when you focus on treasure you can store in heaven, I promise.

Britt

Spending loads of money on material things to be seen as worthy and important is a cheap trade.

51

Your Untidy Heart Is Welcome Here

Offer hospitality to one another without grumbling. Each of you
should use whatever gift you have received to serve others,
as faithful stewards of God's grace in its various forms.

1 PETER 4:9-10

I'm the type of person who is deeply affected by my environment, which means clutter is my kryptonite. I wouldn't say I'm a neat freak, but I do get overwhelmed when my home is in chaos. For a mother of three who works from home, recently moved, released her first book, and began writing the book you're holding in your hands, this is fairly often. With all this going on at once, it's been difficult for me to keep our new home clutter free, let alone unpack and decorate to my heart's content.

I enjoy hosting get-togethers, cookouts, and movie nights and serving good, old-fashioned comfort food, but lately I've been hesitant to invite anyone over. I'm embarrassed to admit it, but I cringe at the thought of unexpected guests. I just want to put a Do Not Enter sign on my front door until I can get my life and home together, but that's not realistic.

Here's the thing: I know deep down that my house doesn't need to be Pinterest perfect for God to use it, even if that would make *me* more comfortable.

Peter taught us to offer hospitality to one another and to use whatever God has given us to serve others (1 Peter 4:9–10). Our home truly is a miraculous gift from God—I call it our "miracle home" because so many things had to line up for us to call it ours!—and offering hospitality is a wonderful way to use what God has given us to serve others.

Dear friend, our homes are sacred spaces where we find beauty in the mundane. Our couches are a resting place for the weary. Our tables are a gathering place for the hungry and discarded.

These days I don't rush to clean up if someone is coming over. I'll wash dishes and fold clothes while I visit with my guests, which offers them an unspoken invitation: *This is a safe place to show your imperfections. Your untidy heart is welcome here.*

Our homes and hearts don't need to be perfect for God to use them. People need to see the messy interiors of our lives; they need to know that God can meet them in the middle of their mess too.

Cass

52

Anchored in Christ, Even in Crisis

"I will never leave you nor forsake you."

HEBREWS 13:5 ESV

If your life is anything like mine, when it rains, it pours.

I've walked through some pretty difficult seasons in the last four years. I've watched a close family member suffer a brain injury and regress to the mental capacity of a child. I battled severe postpartum depression that landed me in the hospital for several days. Needless to say, I'm no stranger to crisis.

And it never fails: at the moment when I feel I've mustered enough strength to climb out of the pit, it's as if the Enemy kicks me right back in. It might be something small, like watching the minuscule details of my day topple like dominos. Or it could be something a bit bigger, like continual bad news that leaves me feeling like nothing will ever go right again.

In these moments of despair and uncertainty, the only thing that keeps my foot from slipping is knowing that Christ is my anchor. He is my safety. His Word stabilizes me from falling under.

You see, when the storm comes, it's not time for me to lose character or hope. It's time for me to drop my anchor, be still before the

Lord, and trust Him. Being anchored in Christ protects me from allowing crisis *around* me to create a crisis *within* me. Hard circumstances don't change who I am, and they certainly don't change God or His goodness.

You may not see Him, but He always has His loving eye on you. Cheek to cheek, like a mother rocking her child to sleep—that's how close He is to you in your pain and distress, nurturing you and protecting you.

If you find yourself in crisis, know this: the storm of crisis cannot overcome you, friend. It can never cloud God's vision of you, and He will never abandon you.

Britt

Being anchored in Christ protects me from allowing crisis around me to create a crisis within me.

God's plan
is (worth
the wait

53

Abundance Is Here

"The thief comes only to steal and kill and destroy; I have
come that they may have life, and have it to the full."

JOHN 10:10

*L*et's talk about something fun: abundance! Or at least it *looks* fun
on the surface.

God's definition of abundance doesn't quite mirror the world's.
It's not scoring a huge haul from Costco or getting a windfall that
boosts your bank account. The "full" life in John 10:10 docsn't guarantee us an easy life or promise us health, wealth, and prosperity.

This is how God defines the abundant life: it's a contented life,
one that securely relies on Him to supply our every need. And lucky
for us, the gospel promises He's going to do just that.

Are you wondering what the abundant life looks like? Let me show
you: in the thick of our weariness, we're emboldened to persevere. As
the pressure mounts at our jobs or in our homes, we suddenly feel a
peace that passes all understanding. When we don't have everything
we want, we look around and see that we have everything—and everyone—we need.

When you feel like you don't have enough resources, whether
that's patience, strength, or even enough available on your credit card
balance, at your disposal, I want you to take a deep breath and imagine

someone whispering this simple phrase into your ear: "Abundance is here." When you're desperate for breakthrough and tired of waiting, whisper, "Abundance is here." When you're weary, wounded, and wandering, say it in your mind: "Abundance is here." See how you feel after. I bet you feel better.

An abundant life isn't a guarantee of one without trouble. It *is* a promise that even if the Enemy tries to steal your joy, kill your confidence, and destroy your peace, Jesus came so that you may have life and have it to the full. So I hope you believe that wherever you are today, abundance can be found. This isn't blind optimism or toxic positivity. This is a simple yet profound truth: the abundance of God isn't reliant upon your circumstances. You can find abundance anywhere if you look for Jesus there.

Cass

God's definition
of abundance
doesn't quite mirror
the world's.

Changing Circumstances
Don't Change His Goodness

Jesus Christ is the same yesterday and today and forever.

HEBREWS 13:8

*W*e've all had the occasional bad days or rough season.
In my experience, it seems that on those days, every inconvenient thing piles on top of one another.

I've had days when I woke up to get ready for work and spilled my coffee, stubbed my toe, put on mismatched shoes, and hit every red light on my way just to walk in the door and have my boss get onto me about something from the day before. Instant adult temper tantrum on my part, pointing my finger at God for my bad day.

Maybe you can relate!

Or how about this: when some unspeakable event happens in your life that causes you immense grief, everything that follows seems to go wrong. This opens the door for far more than a temper tantrum; try a season of depression and anxiety.

Sister, when our circumstances shatter, it's so hard not to do the same ourselves. But when the going gets rough, try to remember this plea: please don't give your circumstances the power to change your view of God—or of yourself. Because when everything falls apart, that's the time to fall before God's feet and take your problems to His throne.

The Enemy will try to use our hardest moments to infiltrate our hearts and cause us to question God's goodness. But we know the truth: "Jesus Christ is the same yesterday and today and forever."

We must rise above our circumstances. Yes, they challenge us, but they don't have to change us. The Enemy wants us to buckle under pressure and question God's goodness. He wants to paint God as a tyrant, and it's simply not true.

As hard as it may be, we need to separate our experiences from what we know to be true about God. His goodness is the same, even on our worst days. We can take our grief to Him and know that regardless of whatever pain we may be walking through, He will work in all situations for our good and His glory (Romans 8:28).

Britt

Please don't give your circumstances the power to change your view of God—or of yourself.

55

Blanket Burritos and Burnout

The Lᴏʀᴅ is my shepherd, I lack nothing. He makes
me lie down in green pastures, he leads me
beside quiet waters, he refreshes my soul.

PSALM 23:1-3

I recently had a dear friend speak some hard truth into my life. She sternly warned me, "You will burn yourself to the ground if no one stops you, and I refuse to watch you burn."

She was right, of course. I was exhausted but I wasn't ready to admit it. Full transparency: I fall into a bad habit of neglecting my needs and denying my limitations when I'm stressed. When that happens, I disconnect from my body too. I can't see what my body needs as it's trying to tell me, "Hey, I'm tired! Hey, I'm stressed! Maybe we need some good food, good fellowship, and some *sleep*." Self-neglect is not helpful at all.

Check, checkity, check. I had hit the trifecta. I was working through lunch, often skipping meals, I wasn't socializing (at all), and I was tossing and turning all night long. Once I recognized there was a problem, I took a break.

What started as a few days turned into a few weeks. During that much-needed pause, I picked up my Bible, turned to Psalm 23 (so comforting when I'm stressed), and learned a few valuable lessons.

1. *God is my shepherd, and I lack nothing* (v. 1). When I feel the pressure to produce as if the burden falls all on me, I'm reminded that in Christ I have everything I need. I'm learning to trust God to lead me by paying compassionate attention to the signals my body gives me. These gentle warnings prompt me to intentionally slow down instead of numbing out and pushing my body beyond its threshold.

2. *God makes me lie down in green pastures, and He leads me beside quiet waters* (v. 2). I love how the Christian Standard Bible translates this verse as "He *lets me* lie down" (emphasis mine). God is a caring and kind Shepherd who allows us to rest in pleasant places, if only we will allow ourselves to move away from the noise and the busyness and get still.

3. *The Lord refreshes my soul* (v. 3). The rest God gives cannot be found in our well-intentioned attempts at self-care. Nothing satisfies our soul's desperate need for renewal like spending time in Christ's tender loving care.

Dear friend, I don't think burnout was the sweet-smelling aroma Paul had in mind in Ephesians 5:2. We're called to worship God not by setting ourselves ablaze upon the altar of productivity, but rather by choosing to honor Him with our work, worshipping Him as we cease striving, and resting in Him.

I want to challenge you to rest in Him today. Step away and schedule a break. Go for a walk. Try drinking water instead of the melted ice in your cold brew. Take a nap. Go ahead and wrap yourself in a blanket burrito (10/10 highly recommend).

Cass

you
make
all things
new

ISAIAH 43:18

56

A Grace That Transforms

*Forget the former things; do not dwell on the past. See, I am
doing a new thing! Now it springs up; do you not perceive it? I am
making a way in the wilderness and streams in the wasteland.*

ISAIAH 43:18-19

When I was pregnant with my daughter, I vividly remember the first time she moved in my womb. I was out to lunch with my husband and gasped as I felt what seemed like a tiny butterfly fluttering its wings across the inner lining of my stomach. It was our sweet daughter, Ariana.

From that moment on, butterflies have been significant to me. Anytime I think of my daughter, I think of a butterfly.

What I didn't realize at the time was that butterflies would symbolize what motherhood would be like for me, foreshadowing the transformation that would take place in me.

I went from caring for just myself and my husband for ten years to now caring for another human being before anyone else. I'm being vulnerable here, but motherhood showed me all sorts of selfishness that was embedded in my character. It was really hard for me to adjust to this new life. Yet I felt God's grace guiding me through this process of transforming me into a mother.

This transformation reminds me of the one that takes place when we accept Christ into our lives and become born again. The old life is gone, and the new life has come—just like a caterpillar that turns into a butterfly or a woman who becomes a mother.

The Bible says that we are transformed by the renewing of our minds (Romans 12:2). So let's take action and actively participate in our transformation by yielding our hearts and minds to God's heart in His Word.

Britt

The old life is gone, and the new life has come—just like a caterpillar that turns into a butterfly.

The Lord Delights in You

The LORD your God is with you, the Mighty Warrior who
saves. He will take great delight in you; in his love he will no
longer rebuke you, but will rejoice over you with singing.

ZEPHANIAH 3:17

When I dedicated my life to Christ, one of the first verses of Scripture I ever memorized was Zephaniah 3:17. "The LORD your God is with you, the Mighty Warrior who saves. He will take great delight in you; in his love he will no longer rebuke you, but will rejoice over you with singing."

Let's break this down, shall we?

There's something really special about knowing that God is with us. He isn't a distant God. He is God within us, through us, and among us. Our mighty Savior just so happens to delight in us with gladness.

Have you ever looked up what it means to delight in someone? I did. It means that someone brings you great joy and satisfaction. And that's how God feels about you, sister. You bring God so much joy just by being you. This might be a difficult concept to accept, but it's true. You're His daughter, and He delights in you.

The last few lines of this verse are my favorite. God no longer condemns us but tenderly embraces us and soothes us instead. He takes it one step further and sings over us. God Himself rejoices over us with singing. I'll forever be in awe of His loving-kindness.

Just like it did when I first read it, this scripture continues to minister to my heart, and the Lord still uses it to meet me with His tender mercy in my times of need.

So let me encourage you: if you're anxious, read Zephaniah 3:17. If you're lonely, read Zephaniah 3:17. If you're depressed, read Zephaniah 3:17. If you need to know you're deeply loved, read Zephaniah 3:17.

Cass

You bring God so much joy just by being you.

Rejection Redirection

He chose us in him, before the foundation of the world, to
be holy and blameless in love before him. He predestined
us to be adopted as sons through Jesus Christ for himself,
according to the good pleasure of his will, to the praise of his
glorious grace that he lavished on us in the Beloved One.

EPHESIANS 1:4-6 csb

There's no doubt about it: rejection just *stings*, doesn't it?

When someone tells us no, it's so hard not to wallow in our disappointment. But what would our lives look like if we allowed each rejection we face to redirect us toward God? Or if we took each closed door to His throne of grace and allowed Him to tenderly care for our hearts, then redirect us to where He intends?

Friend, every no is a sealed invitation to approach God with empty hands and a readiness to follow His lead. A thousand doors could close in your face, but all that matters is that one door will always be open: God's door.

Now, this doesn't mean that rejection won't sting anymore because it absolutely will. But if we aren't careful, we may start to fear the way we feel after a door is closed in our face. We might fear the pain we feel after someone we admire or something we tried so hard to accomplish crumbles right before our eyes. If we are living with a people-pleasing mindset that ties our worth to our accomplishments, then guess what? Receiving a rejection could leave us questioning our purpose—and even our worth. Not good.

If you've been getting no after no, I hope you remember this: your worth is not tied to what you do, and it's not tied to any closing door either. Jesus was rejected more than any person who has walked this earth, yet it did not affect His assignment. God knew what He was doing with His plan for Jesus' life, and He knows what He's doing with yours too.

God's goodness doesn't waver in the face of rejection, and neither does your worth to Him. After all, whenever a door closes, you never know what window He's going to open.

Britt

Every no is a sealed invitation to approach God with empty hands and a readiness to follow His lead.

59

A Word on Weeping

Weeping may stay overnight, but there is joy in the morning.

PSALM 30:5 CSB

Lately I've been reflecting on what a gift it is to mourn alongside those I love. In our hardest moments we wait for miracles and say goodbye at burials. Mourning what used to be. Mourning what never could be. Mourning what we thought should be.

Each in our own time, we've been learning to let go of unmet expectations and prayers that weren't answered the way we hoped. We've leaned into the trust we have in a Father who works things together for our good, somehow, someway. It's hard but holy work.

It's hard enough to mourn together, but I wonder: What would it be like to go through your hardest seasons alone? What would it be like to wait for the doctor to call when you don't have a hand to hold? How would it feel to lose a parent and have no shoulder to cry on?

When David wrote Psalm 30:5, he said, "Weeping may stay overnight, but there is joy in the morning" (CSB). I don't think David *literally* meant you'd be fine the next day. I think he meant that, in time, joy would return to your life. And I believe that when you have other people who can help you carry your grief during those heavy seasons, your heart is lighter, perhaps light enough to let in joy a little earlier than you could have otherwise.

Sister, death still stings on this side of heaven, and weeping might spend the night with you, but it cannot stay forever. Lean on your people during your seasons of need, and believe that joy will find its way back to you one sweet morning.

Cass

It's hard enough to mourn together, but I wonder: What would it be like to go through your hardest seasons alone?

YOU CAN TRUST GOD

60

"I Have Trust Issues"

Commit your way to the Lord; trust in him, and he will act.

PSALM 37:5 ESV

*H*ave you ever had a moment in which you had to place unwavering trust in God? In my experience, in these moments, I'm confronted by the lack of trust I really have.

I find it ironic that we can get into an Uber and trust the driver or get on an airplane and trust the pilot, who are complete strangers, to transport us safely. Yet we have a hard time trusting the One who created us and holds the entire universe in His hands.

I'll be the first to admit that I struggle to trust God. I have trust issues. I like to know what's going to happen and when it's going to happen. I like to be in control, and I feel most comfortable when I have a full understanding of something before I dive into it.

Yet the end of Proverbs 3:5 says, "Do not lean on your own understanding" (ESV), meaning our limited understanding can easily lead us astray.

In Isaiah 55:8, it says, "My thoughts are not your thoughts, neither are your ways my ways, declares the Lord" (ESV) He says it here plain as day: our thoughts are not like His. We do not know what He knows. God sees the whole picture, while we see only our tiny corner of it. Our understanding is so limited in comparison with His.

It's actually a relief to place complete trust in God because when we do, we come into alignment and agreement with His will and His sovereignty. And there's no better, safer place for us to be.

So instead of asking, "How long?" or "Okay, God, but why?" or "When is this going to happen?" instead, try saying, "Yes, God, I trust You."

When doubt creeps in, fill the gap with trust in Him.

When fear causes you to worry, know that He works in all circumstances for your good and for His glory.

Eliminate your need for control, and trust that the Lord will act.

Britt

God sees the whole picture, while we see only our tiny corner of it.

61

Shake off Shame in Jesus' Name

There is now no condemnation for those who are in Christ Jesus.

ROMANS 8:1

One of the most common obstacles we must conquer before we can embrace our true identity in Christ is shame. When we accept Jesus as Lord and Savior of our lives, He cleanses us of our sin, making us pure as white snow (Isaiah 1:18). Many of us know this scripture in our minds, but it's an entirely different concept to accept it in our hearts. I intimately understand this struggle because I've personally been set free from the shackles of the shame of my past.

Dear friend, God wants to free you from the grip of guilt and shame in Jesus' name. The Holy Spirit helps us with this too. He gently nudges us toward godly sorrow over our transgressions, and it's His kindness that leads us to repentance (Romans 2:4).

So if you find it difficult to embrace the forgiveness God's offering you, trust me when I say that you're not alone. I've personally found it hard to accept the mercy and love that God has generously lavished upon me. For years I wrestled with the concept that I could be made new despite all the awful things I've done.

Here's the thing: I know everything I've done. I remember all the shady places I've been. I'm painfully aware of the hurt I've caused other people. And honestly? At times I've been so disgusted with myself. I've found it hard to imagine that I could ever be washed clean of the dirt and grime of all the wrong I've done.

But can I encourage you with something? Despite what the Enemy of your soul will try to tell you, in Christ you can be made new (2 Corinthians 5:17). Your past doesn't hold the power to define you because when you confess your sins, He is faithful to forgive you (1 John 1:9). You don't have to hold on to shame because Jesus took it away.

Isn't that the best news? God knows what He purchased on Calvary, and He has no intention of returning you. You're forgiven. There's nothing that can separate you from the love of God. So live secure in Him today and shake off shame in Jesus' name.

Cass

Despite what the Enemy of your soul will try to tell you, in Christ you can be made new

a bad day
doesn't mean
a bad life

A Bad Day Doesn't
Equal a Bad Life

This is the day the Lord has made. We will rejoice and be glad in it.

PSALM 118:24 NLT

Have you ever had the kind of day when nothing seems to go right? Maybe you got into a bad argument with your spouse or family member. Maybe it's a bunch of little things that keep adding up:

- You got zero sleep because your baby was teething.
- Your old phone keeps freezing up.
- You hit every stoplight while running late.
- You spilled your coffee on your new shirt.
- Your day doesn't go as planned.

These are typically minor issues (and what some call "first-world problems"). But small frustrations can add up, especially if we aren't taking our frustration to God.

I don't know who needs to hear this, but here's a friendly reminder: a bad day doesn't equal a bad life.

Don't allow the Enemy to make you feel like you have a horrible life. The Enemy's goal is to change your mindset from blessed to stressed. But you, my dear, have so many blessings.

He wants you to see everything through a lens of frustration and look for problems, almost like an inspector looking for deficiencies. This is no way to live your life. If you look for problems, then guess what? That's exactly what you'll find. But the opposite is true too: if you look for blessings, you will find them.

So what if you decided that a bad day doesn't equal a bad life and that tomorrow will be better? When you wake up in the morning, what if you said to yourself that "this is the day that the LORD has made; let's rejoice and be glad in it" (Psalm 118:24 CSB).

If you start to have one of those days and catch yourself going into "inspector mode," check yourself. Challenge yourself to count your blessings. Pray and remind God of all the things He has blessed you with. Name three to start, and I bet your day will begin to turn around.

And if all else fails, remember: this, too, shall pass.

Britt

Come as You Are

"Whoever is faithful in very little is also faithful in much, and whoever is unrighteous in very little is also unrighteous in much."

LUKE 16:10 CSB

I recently had a conversation with a friend. We were talking about the importance of honoring God despite our discomfort and how our obedience to Christ often comes at great personal cost. During this conversation my friend reminded me of something I hadn't thought about in a while: if we wait until we're invited to offer our gifts and service to our community, we could miss a divine opportunity to bring God glory because that invitation might never come.

As followers of Jesus, we are called in Colossians 3:23 to show up where we are with what we've got and work as if everything we do is for the Lord. It sounds easy to do on the surface, right? Just use the gifts and tools you already have, and keep your focus on God as you work. But as humans we have a tendency to mess up the things God intended to be simple. We overcomplicate stuff.

The world tells us we need to have more and be more in order to have any influence or do anything that matters. And Lord help us in our social media–saturated world to keep our eyes on Him. When everyone and everything is trying to get our attention, feeding us that false narrative about *more, more, more*—marketers who want our money, influencers who want us to tap affiliate links—it's no wonder God needs to take a second to tell us what really matters as we serve Him: *use what you have, and focus on Me.*

Listen, sister: you don't need to *have* more or *be* more in order to do more. God is watching you in the ordinary moments of your life, when you're beyond the gaze of people and focused on pleasing Him. He sees your kindness when you make a meal for a new mom down the street when your own freezer could've used it. He sees your patience as you referee another Saturday afternoon between your littles as you're trying to relax. He sees your wisdom as you talk with a colleague about a complicated issue with a client, one in which you could've tried to save face by keeping the problem to yourself.

Our faithfulness in these unseen moments is no small thing; it's in these tiny fragments of time when our hearts are seen and our motives are known by God. In fact, Luke 16:10 tell us that the people who can be trusted with a little can be trusted with a lot. Sounds like life's little moments are a proving ground for bigger things.

So I want to challenge you today: just show up where you are with what you have, and keep your focus on Him. You'll never know where life's little moments will lead you when you don't overcomplicate those two little things.

Cass

64

Pick up Your Sword

The word of God is living and active, sharper than any two-edged
sword, piercing to the division of soul and of spirit, of joints and of
marrow, and discerning the thoughts and intentions of the heart.

HEBREWS 4:12 ESV

Imagine playing a professional sport. Now imagine playing that
sport without your equipment: a baseball player without a bat, a
football player without a helmet, or a basketball player without a ball.

No professional would imagine doing their job without the proper
equipment, whether they're an athlete, a chef, or a soldier going into
battle. So why do we as Christians not utilize our special equipment:
our sword of the Spirit, the Word of God?

The Bible has never been more accessible than it is right now.
There are more translations and formats—from audio Bibles to study
Bibles, commentaries, and apps galore—than ever before. Yet so often
we don't go to the Bible for encouragement, wisdom, or comfort when
we need it most.

When Jesus was tempted in the desert, His usual response began
with, "It is written" (Matthew 4:1–11). Everything He faced, He meas-
ured against Scripture. If God didn't say it, then Jesus wasn't going
to do it.

Friend, don't forget: the Word of God not only tells us who we are in Christ, but it's essentially a guide for life. If you want to run the race well, the one the apostle Paul talked about in 1 Corinthians 9:24, then you've got to strengthen yourself with the Word. If you want to fend off the flaming arrows from the Enemy, grab your sword of the Spirit, pick up your shield of faith, and win your battle.

Britt

Why do we as Christians not utilize our special equipment: our sword of the Spirit, the Word of God?

65

Trauma Doesn't Triumph over Truth

He heals the brokenhearted and binds up their wounds.

PSALM 147:3

I recently sat at a table filled with women I respect and adore. Taking turns around the table, we each shared our greatest victories and our deepest heartaches. With tears streaming down our faces, we held space for each other's stories to be told with reverence and we offered each other heartfelt solidarity. That dimly lit patio was a sacred place.

While we shared, I felt pressed to say, "Only share what doesn't cut you on the way out." We all stared at each other, and I knew immediately that was directly from the Holy Spirit because I'm not that eloquent with words. I think what I was trying to communicate was that if we haven't healed from something privately, we must be careful not to inflict further pain upon ourselves by tackling it publicly. As someone who has been diagnosed with a mental health condition called PTSD, I know the importance of processing pain in privacy and safety.

Here are the most painful lies of the Enemy that I combat daily: *Your trauma defines you, and your wounds are the most interesting thing about you.* Because of these lies, I battle the belief that the worst things said to me and the horrible things that have happened to me hold the power to define me. But through the power of the Holy Spirit and extensive trauma-informed therapy, I've been able to dismantle this false belief and confront it with truth.

One of my favorite scriptures that helps me live free from the pain of my past is Psalm 147:3: "He heals the brokenhearted and binds up their wounds." This verse reminds me that the abuse I've endured, the statistics that were stacked against me, and all the flashbacks that have haunted me do not yield the power to define me. There's no amount of suffering I can walk through that His healing hands cannot soothe.

Dear friend, there's healing in the mighty name of Jesus. In Him, your story is made new. In Him, all the worst things that have been spoken over you cease to be true. In Him, your broken heart is mended.

If my story resonates with you, I hope you learn to talk about your healing as much as you discuss your scars. I want to encourage you to process your pain in safety with trustworthy people who will handle you with care. And I hope you'll walk in this truth: Your pain isn't the most interesting thing about you, and trauma doesn't triumph over truth. Even if it's slow going, remember that healing one wound at a time is still healing.

Cass

being who
God made you
to be is so much
better than your
best imitation of
someone else.

66

Authentic over Aesthetic

They loved human praise more than praise from God.

JOHN 12:43

*Y*ears ago I went to a "purse party." Do you remember those? At the time I had never been to one before, but having purse parties and Mary Kay makeup parties was the highlight of the early 2000s, so I had to join in the fun.

When I walked in the host's front door, I immediately saw beautiful "designer" bags staged on a long, white folding table. Knowing the bags were discounted, I stood in bewilderment, wondering which bag to grab and examine for my purchase. I then picked up a black leather "Chanel" handbag with gold and leather woven through the straps.

From afar it looked like a real Chanel, but when I got up close, I quickly realized that the leather was faux. If the fifty-dollar price tag didn't give it away, everything about this bag was fake from top to bottom. It smelled like plastic, it didn't feel or look like real leather, and the stitching was barely put together at the seams.

What did I do next? I purchased it. Surely nobody else would know that it was fake unless they held it in their hands. I wanted to be thought of as someone who could afford a designer bag, so a fifty-dollar price tag seemed like a worthy trade to be viewed as important and successful.

I carried this bag around school proudly for the next week, but my pride was quickly squashed when the strap broke and my purse fell to the ground. Standing in embarrassment, I looked down at my broken, fake Chanel purse. Though it had a Chanel logo and the appearance of an authentic bag, everything about it was cheap and doomed to fall apart within a few uses. And that's exactly what happened.

I wasted my money on basically a trash bag so that others would view me as worthy for having it. I traded authenticity for something aesthetically pleasing to others, even though it was worse quality than a fifteen-dollar Walmart purse.

How often do we do things like this? We trade being authentically ourselves for what's aesthetically pleasing to others. The problem is that our best imitation of what others want us to be will always fall short in comparison to the person God created us to be.

Which brand is better than the One who created you in His image? The One who created the heavens and earth created you in His likeness? You can't "knock" that off. And once you live securely in this truth, you will be empowered to show up as your true, authentic self. You won't need to grab ahold of anything else, even the opinions of others, to validate you.

You are so much more than just a knockoff. You are uniquely designed in the image of God.

Britt

67

When You're Not Sure
Which Way to Go

Trust in the LORD with all your heart and lean not on
your own understanding; in all your ways submit to
him, and he will make your paths straight.

PROVERBS 3:5-6

I have an inconvenient habit of getting lost, especially when I'm in a
new city, which is why I avoid taking road trips by myself. I always
try to rope someone into my shenanigans because I know that when
I'm left to my own devices, I'll always end up somewhere I didn't
intend to go.

Similarly, when the only guide we consult for our lives is our
own intuition, our vision is impaired. We're bound to get lost and
travel down roads we never intended to go because we didn't use the
ultimate GPS: the Word. Only God can be trusted to guide us down
the right path.

If you've found yourself lost and wandering, God's love and wis-
dom can always guide you home. No matter how far you've wandered,
He has never lost sight of you. So trust Him with all your heart today.
He will direct your path, one surrendered step at a time.

Cass

68

Hold God's Opinion Higher

Without faith it is impossible to please him, for whoever
would draw near to God must believe that he exists
and that he rewards those who seek him.

HEBREWS 11:6 ESV

This is a complete understatement, but here we go: the world offers us a lot of opinions.

One post on social media opens a fire hose to the unsolicited opinions and comments of the billions logging onto the internet on any given day. It can feel like you're in a fishbowl, to be honest. In fact, more than ever I feel like we're all logging on and fearing how other people may view us if we do or say the wrong thing.

But imagine this for a second:

You walk into the grocery store, and as you make your way through the produce section, you see someone you don't know. You've never met this person before; they're a complete stranger. Then they come up to you and start attacking your character, shouting that you never do what you say you're going to do. This would normally be upsetting, but you immediately think to yourself, *You don't know me. How can you say that about me when you've never met me?*

If you're like me, you'd shrug it off and laugh that a complete stranger would ever try to tell you the first thing about you.

Now think of that scenario again, but swap the stranger for someone who knows you well. Actually, let's swap that person for Jesus. I think we'd receive that scenario a bit differently, don't you? Since He knows everything about you, if He told you the same things the stranger did, Jesus would be speaking absolute truth.

Now, I don't think our Lord Jesus would attack your character, but do you see how much value we assign to the words and relationships in which we are truly known?

Since He knows you so well, let's think about the wonderful things God says about you in His Word. He calls you His child. Among many things, He says that you're blessed, restored, redeemed, and more than a conqueror.

Seems even sillier to give weight to a bunch of strangers' opinions, doesn't it?

Sister, allow Jesus' words to hold the greatest weight in your mind, and refuse to allow the opinions of strangers to make you fearful. People will always have their opinions, but you know what? Those opinions are none of your concern, and you're not here to please them anyway. Let's decide to hold God's opinion higher than anyone else's.

Britt

69

When Work Becomes Your Worth

Commit to the LORD whatever you do, and
he will establish your plans.

PROVERBS 16:3

*W*hen I think about the job I get to do, sometimes I pinch myself. Five years ago all I wanted to do was write encouraging words, point people to their identity in Jesus, and contribute to my household financially. Now I'm an author, speaker, and coleader of the Her True Worth community, serving millions of women all over the world.

I love what I do. But it's not who I am. I know my Father would love me just as much no matter what my job title might be.

Listen, I'm all for working hard and honoring God with the work of our hands. That's one of the most gratifying parts of my life! But the "girl boss" culture taking over our lives—telling us that we always need to be doing more, reaching more, earning more—is selling us a lie. If we believe our worth comes from what we do, what we earn or who we reach, before long we become hooked on the hustle and striving for success in an attempt to earn our worth.

Sister, don't forget: you don't have to *do* more to *be* more. You have nothing to prove. Your Father loves you for the kind, smart, creative, funny, committed human being you already are.

So let's continue to smash glass ceilings without crushing ourselves in the process. It's possible to respect the hustle without worshipping it. Our work matters, but it's not what matters most.

Cass

Sister, don't forget: you don't have to do more to be more.

70

Dehydrated Faith

O God, you are my God; earnestly I seek you; my
soul thirsts for you; my flesh faints for you, as in a
dry and weary land where there is no water.

PSALM 63:1 ESV

Have you ever gone through a dry season? A time when you were stagnant and not growing spiritually? I have. I went from my cup running over to becoming as dry as the desert in the blink of an eye.

I remember the moment I realized how dry my faith had become and how dehydrated I felt. At the time I wasn't quite sure what had happened or how I had gotten to that point. To make matters worse, I felt like God wasn't close to me anymore. It seemed like He wasn't listening and as if He was extremely far away.

The term *drought* is defined as: "a prolonged absence of something specified; thirst."[4]

Looking back, I can see that my spiritual growth was stunted by not pursuing God daily. So what happens in a prolonged absence from spending time in God's presence and Word? We become spiritually dry. And when we become spiritually dehydrated, *nothing* will quench our souls better than the living water: Jesus.

In seasons of drought, if you aren't going to the One who is Living

Water, then you may find yourself feeling dehydrated and drinking from the wells of the world to hydrate. That's a problem because the wells of the world will never quench your thirst and satisfy your soul. You'll always be thirsty.

So if you're in a spiritual drought right now, I implore you to dive into God's Word and spend time in quiet prayer. Go to the well where you'll receive not only an abundance of water, but the Living Water that'll satisfy your soul.

Britt

What happens in a prolonged absence from spending time in God's presence and Word? We become spiritually dry.

YOUR BODY
IS A VESSEL TO
BE NURTURED,
NOT A VILLAIN
TO BE CONQUERED.

Your Body Isn't a Villain

Do you not know that your bodies are temples of the Holy Spirit, who is in you, whom you have received from God? You are not your own; you were bought at a price. Therefore honor God with your bodies.

1 CORINTHIANS 6:19-20

I know this might sound shallow, but I've struggled with looking for my worth on the scale. I can't tell you how many years I've battled the false belief that my value as a woman directly correlates with the size of my jeans. But the sad thing is, I know I'm not the only one.

We live in a culture obsessed with obtaining the ideal body, and this damaging narrative found its way into my mind long before I hit puberty. The earliest memory I have of someone critiquing my body was when I was six years old. The experience is etched in my mind as a negative core memory. It was the day my mother married my loving stepfather. Participating in their wedding, I was feeling so special as I twirled in my elegant, white dress until a male family member pinched the side of my belly and said, "Look at that baby fat. You might be a bit too chubby to be wearing that." His brief comment crushed my tiny heart. And after that, the critic within me kept chipping away at my confidence for many years to come.

There's an entire industry that exploits our desire to obtain the

157

perfect body and profits on our pain, and when I was younger, I was right in its clutches. I abused my body in my attempt to starve it into submission. I dedicated all my time, energy, and money into achieving the goal of seeing that magic number on the scale.

It breaks my heart to think about how the world trained me to treat my body as if it were my enemy instead of the trusted friend who has helped me climb trees, healed skinned knees, shared date-night pizza with the man who would become my husband, and even had the strength to bring my children into this world.

Sweet friend, our bodies are vessels to be nurtured and protected, not villains to be conquered. In addition to the wonderful things our bodies have brought us through, Paul reminded us in 1 Corinthians 6:19–20 that they have an even bigger purpose: they are the dwelling place of the Holy Spirit. We each carry a piece of the divine right where we are, sitting in our favorite easy chair and wearing our favorite yoga pants.

Sister, don't forget: the number on the scale doesn't define you, and it definitely doesn't dictate your worth. God has already done that for you. And He's made your body a place where His Spirit dwells, a place where you can be His hands and feet to a world who needs His love.

Cass

72

The Devil Who Distracts Us

I am saying this for your own good, not to restrict you, but that
you may live in a right way in undivided devotion to the Lord.

1 CORINTHIANS 7:35

The first time I ever used TikTok, I was shocked at how quickly I
got sucked into it. With a simple swipe of the thumb, I could be
endlessly entertained for hours, from learning how to build the perfect
home aesthetic to having my own curated playlist of videos. It can
easily become a time-waster as our lives ticktock away. And here's what
really gets me: I find it perplexing how much easier it is to spend four
hours on social media than it is to spend four hours in God's Word.

Time is one resource that's in limited supply because we never get
it back. Each of us gets 1,440 minutes per day to steward.

It's critical to spend our time wisely. Why? Because if the Enemy
cannot have our hearts, he'll do his best to distract us. And if we are
spending our time distracted, then we aren't spending our time com-
muning with Jesus and we aren't making an impact for the kingdom.

Let's aim to live our lives undistracted for Jesus.

Britt

73

Breaking Free from Busy

You will keep in perfect peace those whose minds
are steadfast, because they trust in you.

ISAIAH 26:3

I have something to tell you: I have a bad habit of wearing busyness as if it were a badge of honor.

We see hard work praised in our world and even in Scripture (Colossians 3:23–24 comes to mind, for sure). But when we equate our work with our worth, we find ourselves in danger of developing an idol. You might be wondering, *What's an idol?* An idol is basically anyone or anything that we worship other than God.

The first Christian nonfiction book I ever read was *Breaking Free* written by the trailblazing preacher and teacher Beth Moore. In *Breaking Free* Moore wrote about what she called "the captivity of activity,"[5] where good works can actually hinder our walk with God when we allow ourselves to become consumed by *doing* for God instead of *being* with God.

Hello, conviction! I'm spilling my own tea here. I've personally found myself hooked on the hustle and striving to earn my worth through the work of my hands. There have been so many seasons when I've found it hard to take a pause and simply rest my body and mind.

When we find ourselves struggling to rest, it's good to examine our hearts and ask, *Do I truly trust God? Do I believe He loves me aside from what I do? Will He provide for me when my body can't do anymore?*

Sweet friend, there are so many Scripture promises that can show you how worthy He is of your trust.

Isaiah 40:31 says that God will give you strength when you don't have more to give.

Ephesians 2:8–9 reminds us that we've been saved by grace. And we didn't earn that grace; it's God's gift to us.

Proverbs 3:5–6 instructs us to lean on God, not on ourselves, and that He'll point us in the right direction if we continually look to Him.

Today is a great day to break free from striving and cast off the badge of busyness once and for all. We don't have to produce or perform to find peace. God offers it freely to those whose trust is in Him.

Cass

God restores the wounded heart.

God Restores the Wounded Heart

The LORD is near to the brokenhearted and saves the crushed in spirit.

PSALM 34:18 ESV

At some point in our lives, we will encounter a situation that causes our hearts to break and sends us to our knees.

Whenever I've dealt with a broken heart in the past, it seemed that nothing would be able to fix it. Whether it was grief from a breakup or losing something or someone, the pain was almost always too much to bear. What once felt like normal life quickly felt like an excruciatingly painful one.

Postpartum was a rough period for me, one in which I felt extremely vulnerable all the time. I struggled with postpartum anxiety and depression, and the loss of my healthy mental state left me feeling broken. I felt fragile, afraid, and worried that I was losing my mind. On top of it all, I was in so much pain because I was unable to truly bond and be present with my new daughter.

But even then, the Holy Spirit instilled the confidence in me that God can make any broken thing new again, that He could heal my mind and bring balance back to my body.

Just like a brilliant potter gently restoring a fragile, broken pot, He, too, handles us with such care. Most often God does His best healing and restoration when our hearts are broken and vulnerable.

Sometimes we try and mend our brokenness ourselves. We turn to things that make us feel whole. But if we turn to anything other than God, we will never find true healing. If we don't handle our wounds, our wounds will handle us.

I honestly believe that we are closest to God when we're standing in the aftermath of our hearts being shattered into a million pieces. In our despair, we have to cling to Him like never before. We have to trust Him like never before.

If you are in a state of brokenness and despair right now, know this: what broke you does not hold the power to destroy you. Jesus said, "Blessed are those who mourn, for they will be comforted" (Matthew 5:4). If your heart needs to be mended, go to God. Watch Him carefully and powerfully take your heart and restore it into something beautiful and whole in Him.

Britt

75

Surrender Your Plans

We know that in all things God works for the good of those who
love him, who have been called according to his purpose.

ROMANS 8:28

I have an annoying tendency of having to learn things the hardest possible way. These life lessons tend to be a reflection of my lack of experience or my own sinful choices. I've flunked a few of life's hardest lessons a few times. It stings to admit that.

I'm someone who likes to have a plan. I like to know what's happening, and I like to know when it's going to happen. So you can imagine how frustrating it can be when life doesn't exactly go according to my plan (heavy emphasis on "my plan"). Slowly but surely, I'm learning to trust God's ways above my own, seeking His kingdom first and letting go of what I think should happen.

Take it from me: there's safety in surrendering your plans to God. There's an abundant life beyond learning everything the hard way (John 10:10). Even when we insist on doing things our own way (and making a mess in the process), He is faithful to work in all situations for the good of those who love Him.

Cass

My Creator
defines my
worth, not
His creation

76

If You're Feeling Not Enough, Read This

Each time he said, "My grace is all you need. My power works best in weakness." So now I am glad to boast about my weaknesses, so that the power of Christ can work through me.

2 CORINTHIANS 12:9 NLT

*I*f you're anything like me, then you've wallowed in the sea of "not enough" for your whole life. You might've used comparison to others and culture as your measuring stick of your "enoughness," yet you've always missed the mark.

Not thin enough.

Not pretty enough.

Not smart enough . . .

The list goes on.

But what if God never intended for us to fit into this stringent world where "enough" is defined by a culture that has little to no desire for Him?

Maybe we have to change our definition of the word *enough*.

The truth is—and this is a hard one, so hear me out for a second—we are *not* enough. If we were enough on our own, then we would have no need for a Savior.

"I am not enough" may sound like a harsh statement, but it's actually a blessing. It's a relief because we don't have to try to be enough once we acknowledge that we need Jesus.

When we acknowledge that we need Jesus, then we can come to a place where we're able to boast in our weakness and allow the power of Christ to work in us and through us.

Without Christ, we are not enough.

In Christ, we are made new, redeemed, righteous, set apart, and forgiven.

Dear friend, you weren't created to define your enoughess by our culture's standards. Don't let yourself fall into that trap any longer. End your striving, and know that in Christ and through His grace, you don't have to try to be enough. He is all you need. Look to Him to define who you are and where you stand in this world.

Britt

If we were enough on our own, then we would have no need for a Savior.

77

When You Need to Course Correct

No temptation has overtaken you except what is common to mankind. And God is faithful; he will not let you be tempted beyond what you can bear. But when you are tempted, he will also provide a way out so that you can endure it.

1 CORINTHIANS 10:13

*H*ave you ever found yourself in a situation that seemed harmless on the surface, but little by little, it led you toward temptation? Here's where I slowly raise my hand and admit . . . I have.

That's the tricky thing about temptation: it's often disguised as a distraction or wrapped in a sneaky cloak of deception. This is why we need to be mindful of situations that might lead to a moment when we could be tempted.

People often say that the road to hell is paved with good intentions. I agree, but I'd like to add this: when we compromise our values one small step at a time, I think those steps are actually leading us closer to the destruction of our divine identity.

That sounds a bit heavy, doesn't it? But the good thing is, if you're on that path, you don't have to stay there. If you let Him, God will lovingly nudge you and redirect you when you're going the wrong way. The conviction of the Holy Spirit will tenderly guide you toward repentance.

Heads up: the devil may try to convince you that you've made too many wrong turns and you've traveled down too many winding roads to turn back now. But that's not true! You're never too far gone. When you're ready to go to Him, God is always there to course correct and lead you toward the right path.

Cass

If you let Him, God will lovingly nudge you and redirect you when you're going the wrong way.

78

God Sees What We Cannot

This is what the high and exalted One says—he who lives forever, whose name is holy: "I live in a high and holy place, but also with the one who is contrite and lowly in spirit, to revive the spirit of the lowly and to revive the heart of the contrite."

ISAIAH 57:15

*H*ave you ever heard that we view time in a linear way? This means we look at the past, present, and future as falling in a straight line. (PS: that's why it's called a *timeline*.) We don't see the entire picture because we're living in only one segment of the line at a time: the present, though sometimes our minds visit different parts of the timeline. We are reminded of the past, sometimes even haunted by it. And we have hope for the future or maybe sometimes worry about it.

Something I find fascinating about God is that He doesn't see a straight timeline like we do. He can stand back far enough to see the entire picture. That's one of the many reasons we can trust Him with our lives: because He sees it all.

For example, if you were standing on the street watching a parade, you would experience each event of the parade as it passed you by. But someone up above the parade—say, a helicopter or even those lucky people who snag a hotel room high above the Macy's Thanksgiving

Day Parade in New York—would be able to see the beginning, middle, and end of the parade all at the same time. That's kind of how God can see everything. He isn't viewing our lives within our perspective of time. He sees it from above on His throne.

And here's something else: He not only sees it all, but He holds it all together. He's above us, behind us, ahead of us, and around us, and He meant it when He said He would make a way (Isaiah 43:16).

I don't know about you, but knowing this gives me a deeper peace within my heart that says, *He's got me.* He truly does know better than I do because He sees what I cannot.

So tonight, rest with peace, knowing that you may not see all the details or know all of the whys, but that in all situations God is working for your good and for His glory.

Britt

That's one of the many reasons we can trust Him with our lives: because He sees it all.

79

Seasons of Comfort

Praise be to the God and Father of our Lord Jesus Christ, the
Father of compassion and the God of all comfort, who comforts
us in all our troubles, so that we can comfort those in any
trouble with the comfort we ourselves receive from God.

2 CORINTHIANS 1:3-4

I was sitting on my couch when my phone rang and a familiar name
filled the screen. And before I picked up the call, I paused and said
a simple prayer: "Lord, help me. Guide my words, and give me ears
to truly hear. Use me to offer the comfort only You can give. Amen."

For this dear friend, my phone number is on a list of people she
calls when she needs support. Her year has been turbulent, and I've
watched her physical health decline without explanation as she's
fiercely advocated for herself. She's endured the dismissal of trusted
health-care providers and been wounded by well-intentioned loved
ones who don't know how to sit with her in the discomfort of sorrow
and uncertainty. This, combined with her waning quality of life, has
had a devastating impact on her mental health.

I'll be the first to admit that comforting someone in their suffering is difficult. I won't pretend that I understand the depth of my
friend's despair, but what I do know is that I can sit with her while
she's there.

If you've ever felt like you're a burden for carrying burdens, I want you to know something: you're not too difficult to love or support. Sometimes the people we love just don't know how to show up for us in our moments of need. On top of that, the Enemy will try to convince us that we're the only ones who have ever felt this way, that we're only worthy of love when we're not burdensome and aren't asking our loved ones for support. But that's simply not true.

We're going to endure many hard seasons. That's just the way life is this side of heaven. But the beautiful thing is that God didn't make us to endure our burdens alone. There's a scripture in Ecclesiastes 4 that says, "Two are better than one, because . . . if either of them falls down, one can help the other up" (vv. 9–10). Did you see that? Not only are we going to have seasons in which we will be the friend doing the helping, but we're going to have some seasons in which we'll be the friend who needs help. Both have their place. Both have their role.

You won't always have the right words; you're going to get it wrong sometimes. But don't let the messiness keep you from showing up for the people who need you. And don't let shame tell you that you're too big of a burden to reach out for help.

But maybe you don't have that kind of friend. Then sister, I want you to remember that Jesus is your best friend, and He's always there to comfort you in your suffering. He will never tire of your tears, and He is always available to hear the aches of your heart.

If you're in need of comfort today, please feel empowered in love to reach out to a friend—and to Him. If someone you love is in need of an empathic ear, wrap her in your arms, and point her to the comfort she can find in Him.

Cass

WHEN YOU
FIND YOURSELF
LOST, YOU ARE
NOT LOVED
ANY LESS

When You're Lost, You're Not Loved Less

I am convinced that neither death nor life, neither
angels nor demons, neither the present nor the future,
nor any powers, neither height nor depth, nor anything
else in all creation, will be able to separate us from
the love of God that is in Christ Jesus our Lord.

ROMANS 8:38-39

I went on a hiking trip several years back with my mom and my friend Melissa. The hike was just for us ladies, and we were thrilled to test our womanly strength on the trails by carrying our own packs. We set out on our three-day, ten-mile hike in northern Michigan with excitement and enthusiasm.

Five miles into our hike, we were having a good old time joking, reminiscing, and admiring the beauty of the great outdoors. Then it all came to an abrupt halt.

"Oh shoot, I think we've been going in the wrong direction!" my mom anxiously shouted.

The look of worry on her face made my stomach drop. I knew we had to be lost, and come to find out, we had gone three miles off the trail. A while before this discovery, I remember thinking the "trail" looked a little uninhabited and untouched by other hikers, but I brushed off the thought. *This is the wilderness,* I said to myself. *It all looks like this.*

On top of being lost, we were also running out of water. And just like that, what once was a fun, enjoyable trip quickly became a worrisome experience as we tried to find our way. But thankfully, after prayer and a few hours of backtracking, we eventually found our way back to the trail.

To me, this story is always a perfect illustration of what happens when we find ourselves lost in life, wandering around with no direction. On our hiking trip we were so distracted by our conversation that we forgot to make sure we knew where we were going. Similarly, when we have too many distractions in our lives and we aren't rooted in Christ, we can quite easily wander off His path.

But here's the good news: though you may be lost, you can find your way back to Him at any time. All you have to do is ask for His help. He doesn't love you any less for wandering away. And as you set off on the trails of life, He'll be your guide, your direction, and the One who gives you purpose.

Britt

Hand over Your Heavy Baggage

Cast your cares on the Lord and he will sustain you;
he will never let the righteous be shaken.

PSALM 55:22

That looks heavy."

My best friend and I were dragging our luggage through the airport on our way to check it at the counter, and she was eyeing my bag with concern.

"Nah," I said, shrugging. As I dragged the bag across the terminal, I began to wonder if *maybe* I had slightly overpacked, but I wasn't willing to admit I needed help. I tried to act like I wasn't straining as I tossed my bag onto the weighing station, but there was no denying it: I was carrying a heavy load, and I was relieved to let it go before proceeding to our gate.

The luggage I was carrying was a minor inconvenience, but I can't help but notice how my stubbornness in this situation parallels my defiant heart in the middle of most difficult seasons.

Have you ever found yourself struggling to admit to the weight of the burdens you carry? Worried that if the people in your life knew how heavy they were, they'd see *you* as a burden? I've totally been there.

If you've found yourself in a similar situation, can I encourage you? Jesus is a friend who will never cast you aside when life gets heavy. I love the fact that Psalm 55:22 tells us to cast our cares on the Lord, and He will sustain us. The promise here is that although we will have difficulties in this world, we can give them to God, and He will carry us through. This scripture doesn't promise us a problem-free life, but it does encourage us that we will never carry the weight of our troubles alone.

Sister, we cannot muscle through life in our own strength. What a relief it is to know that we don't have to bear the burdens of life on our own!

Cast your cares on Him today, and He will sustain you. God can take the baggage you are carrying if you'd just hand it over.

Cass

Jesus is a friend who will never cast you aside when life gets heavy.

The Praise Test

Fire tests the purity of silver and gold, but a
person is tested by being praised.

PROVERBS 27:21 NLT

It doesn't matter whether you're receiving too much or too little—praise has a tendency to test your heart.

Cass and I had just celebrated our first book's launch party, and it was such a blessing. But to be honest, it felt kind of funny to be praised for something I could only give God credit for. Cass and I worked hard to write our book, of course, but God did so much more than we were capable of doing; all I can do is boast that I did my part through my weakness, and His strength was made complete through me. If I'd have let myself absorb all the praise, then I would've become self-absorbed and egotistical about my own ability when really it was Christ in me who helped me along.

Our hearts are tested when we position ourselves on a deserving-of-praise pedestal when, really, God should always get the glory for every good thing in our lives. Like James 1:17 reminds us, "Every good and perfect gift is from above."

So when we boast about the Lord and give Him all the praise, there should be no moments of, "Yeah, but . . ."

It's all about Him.

He gets the glory.

He is to be honored and praised.

Yes, we work hard for Him.

We *get* to work hard because He gave us the ability to do so, but it is only by obedience to what He has said and ordained.

Exalt Him and His name only.

We were not meant to sit on the throne of our own lives.

Britt

Praise has a tendency to test your heart.

If You're Longing to Belong

Accept one another, then, just as Christ accepted
you, in order to bring praise to God.

ROMANS 15:7

It feels so good to belong, doesn't it?

But I'll admit, there was a time in my life when I was so desperate to fit in that I was willing to change who I was to gain the acceptance of others. I went to extreme lengths in an attempt to break into the group of people I wanted to become friends with. I thought if I could look like them, act like them, and talk like them, I'd eventually become one of them. I tried buying the bougie clothes they wore, I attempted to lose my northern accent in order to blend in, and I resorted to disordered eating in an attempt to make myself smaller, literally. Unfortunately, the harder I tried to fit in to places where I didn't belong, the more pain and rejection I experienced. Like my son's scattered puzzle pieces that clutter my office floor, I was a mess—and I couldn't force myself into spaces I wasn't created for.

I hope this goes without saying, but just in case it doesn't: you don't have to alter who you are to find acceptance. Some people will never accept you, which I know is hard to hear. But here's the good news: God will guide you to the people and places where you belong. He did that for me. Because when I stopped striving to fit in, I realized it wasn't the group's approval that I needed. My desire to belong was never about them, not really. It was always about being found in Him and in the community He could provide for me. And sometimes that looks like creating spaces yourself where others can find belonging.

What do you think the world would look like if we embraced each other the way that Christ embraces us, if we celebrated our differences as the beautiful and intentional ways in which He designed us, instead of viewing them as divisive or disruptive? As believers, this type of community is possible. Romans 15:7 prompts us to praise God by offering each other the unconditional acceptance we receive from Jesus.

So don't forget: your value doesn't rise and fall based upon the acceptance of others. You don't have to live your life trying to fit in; you already have the only approval you'll ever need as His cherished daughter. When you rest in His approval, you can create spaces of belonging in His name to share His love and welcome others.

Cass

84

Counterfeiting the Gifts of God

Satan himself masquerades as an angel of light.

2 CORINTHIANS 11:14

*E*xperts estimate there are around $100 million of counterfeit US dollars in circulation at any given time.[6] This means there's a strong chance that you've come across one and didn't know it. A good counterfeit is so close to the real thing that the untrained eye can't tell the difference.

Our Enemy, the devil, is a master counterfeiter. He knows that God has given us good gifts and equipped us with all we need for life and godliness (2 Peter 1:3). The Enemy has heavily invested in making counterfeits for everything God has blessed us with. He does this to attack our identity, throw us off course, and convince us to doubt God's ways.

Take, for example, the gift of sex within marriage. It is a blessing and given to us for procreation and enjoyment. So what does the Enemy do? He twists, turns, and perverts it into a selfish, toxic, harmful culture of hookups, friends with benefits, and one-night stands.

The Enemy spreads counterfeits in other ways too.

God blesses; the Enemy curses.

God made us in His image; the Enemy says, "Not good enough. Get cosmetic surgery."

God gave the gift of prophecy and word of knowledge; the Enemy uses psychics and palm readers.

The list could go on.

Staying in God's Word and being aware of the Enemy's schemes will help you avoid his pitfalls. Don't settle for cheap counterfeits. Wrap yourself in the true gifts that God has given you.

Britt

Our Enemy, the
devil, is a master
counterfeiter.

MY
STRENGTH
COMES
FROM
THE
LORD

85

Embrace Your Weakness

My flesh and my heart may fail, but God is the
strength of my heart, my portion forever.

PSALM 73:26

I'm fortunate to have people in my life who check on me and my spiritual well-being. Lately the question I've been asked most frequently is, "How's your heart?" And to be honest, I hesitate to answer every single time.

My heart has been in a tender place for a while. I know I can trust the people checking on me. I know their motives are pure. But after living through so much trauma, it's really difficult for me to access that level of vulnerability with myself, let alone with others.

Whenever I get a "How's your heart?" text, I pause and deeply consider my response. I wonder how honest I should be, and I wrestle with the instinct to conceal my weakness. Fear tells me that it's dangerous to allow myself to be fully seen and points out that sharing my heart is risky. It reminds me of the times in the past when I've done this and been hurt. But lately when I notice fear whispering in my ear, I try to remember that God promised us His grace is sufficient for us, and His power is made perfect in our weakness (2 Corinthians 12:9). And when my flesh and my heart fail, He promised to be my strength and my portion forever.

(Psalm 73:26 CSB). That's enough to help me be brave, even when I'm scared to be vulnerable.

I recently received a "How's your heart?" text, and this was my response:

> God has been humbling me lately. I've come to the difficult realization that I'm not enough, and I'll never be able to handle life with my own strength. But I'm learning that Jesus really is enough for me.

My friend quickly replied, thanking me for my honesty. She also admitted she had been struggling in her faith but that watching me walk with God had renewed her hope.

Cue the ugly tears. I had no idea what my friend was walking through. That's the beauty of vulnerability. When we're willing to embrace our weakness, God points us to His strength. Paul instructed us to boast gladly in our weaknesses so that God's power can be made evident in us (2 Corinthians 12:9–10). And now I think I know why.

Cass

86

Breaking Up with Being Liked

Just as we have been approved by God to be entrusted
with the gospel, so we speak, not to please man,
but to please God who tests our hearts.

1 THESSALONIANS 2:4 ESV

The desire to be liked isn't inherently evil.

Listen, friend, God wired us to seek approval, but where we go wrong is when we seek it in the wrong places. Because the fact remains: only One can really approve us, and His approval is enough.

But even when we know all of that, we still like to be liked.

Make no mistake; it's kind of like being in a toxic relationship you just can't quit. For whatever reason, we keep coming back. Even our friends and family know this is a bad relationship for us, but still here we are.

But what if—what if—we were okay leaving that toxic relationship? What if we said, "It's not you; it's me"? And broke up. For good.

What if we were okay with being single in this breakup? The version of single that means we don't depend on the approval of others to stand confidently in who we are?

Today is a good day to break up with our toxic relationship with "being liked" and lay down the burden of carrying other people's opinions.

Britt

When You're Under Pressure

We are hard pressed on every side, but not crushed;
perplexed, but not in despair; persecuted, but not
abandoned; struck down, but not destroyed.

2 CORINTHIANS 4:8-9

Have you ever used an Instant Pot? It's one of my favorite ways to get dinner on the table quickly on a busy weeknight. It's crazy to me how I can throw in some chicken, veggies, and potatoes, and a few minutes later we can end up with a delicious soup, all because those ingredients spent a few minutes under pressure.

You've probably heard someone say, "This is a pressure-cooker situation," usually when they feel as though they're being pressed on all sides and they're looking for a release valve. I know I have.

But here's the thing: God can use these moments of pressure to produce something good in our lives, kind of like that delicious weeknight soup. When we walk through adversity, we become resilient and establish a sincere faith that can persevere through any trial. But there's also a different kind of pressure, one that comes from the Enemy, who intends to "sift [us] as wheat" and destroy us (Luke 22:31).

I'm going to be honest with you. Sometimes it's hard for me to tell the difference between these situations. Maybe you can relate.

When the purpose of the pressure we endure in life is unclear, it's important that we consider what the pressing is producing. In times like this, try to ask yourself: *Is this experience building me up or attempting to tear me down? Is this producing good fruit in my life? Is this pressing the fruit of the Spirit out of me, or am I reacting with anger, frustration, fear, and bitterness?* What the pressure produces within us and through us can help us to determine the source of the pressure being applied.

When the pressure of life feels like it's more than I can bear, I turn to 2 Corinthians 4:8–9 to encourage my weary heart: "We are hard pressed on every side, but not crushed; perplexed, but not in despair; persecuted, but not abandoned; struck down, but not destroyed."

The Enemy wants to shake our faith and crush us under the weight of discouragement, but God already holds the victory. What a relief it is to know that even when we're struck down, God won't allow the Enemy to destroy us. It's in our difficulty that God can cultivate the resilience we need to persevere through adversity and produce His good work through us.

Sister, I'm not sure what you're walking through today, but here's what I do know: we can endure the pressing, no matter what kind, when we're in His presence.

Cass

Changing out Our Labels

He said to her, "Daughter, your faith has
made you well; go in peace."

LUKE 8:48 ESV

*H*ave you ever felt so broken that you lost all hope of ever being
healed or freed from your pain? I know I have. I went through
a difficult mental health crisis during my postpartum period after the
birth of our daughter. I felt afraid that I would have to live in a state
of broken mental health for the rest of my life. In my brokenness I had
to cling to Jesus like never before.

And in my pain, I was comforted by the faith of the woman in
the Gospel of Luke who had a horrible blood issue that lasted well
over a decade.

This woman, who was rejected by all around her, had been hemorrhaging for twelve years and was considered "unclean" in her society.
She was unable to touch anyone or be around them, so she remained
hidden from everyone.

As Jesus made His way through a crowd of people who were seeking His healing, she, too, made her way to Him, hoping one touch
of His cloak would heal her. She got her chance. She reached out and
touched His cloak. He felt power leave from Him and asked, "Who
touched Me?" (Luke 8:45).

Luke went on to say, "The woman, seeing that she could not go unnoticed, came trembling and fell at his feet. In the presence of all the people, she told why she had touched him and how she had been instantly healed. Then he said to her, 'Daughter, your faith has healed you. Go in peace'" (Luke 8:47–48).

As a woman labeled unclean by society, her behavior suggests she felt it was considered unacceptable to come to Jesus, openly risking being seen by others. Yet He not only healed her, but He brought her into the open and changed her label from outcast to daughter.

How often do we label ourselves as unclean, unworthy, or dirty? Yet, at the same time, the love of Christ calls us away from those broken labels, bringing us into a state of wholeness in Him.

I learned from this story that nothing is beyond Jesus' repair. He sees my uncleanliness and still calls me daughter. Even when I feel like an outcast, He still looks at me with love.

The same is true for you, friend.

The lie is that you will never find healing, hope, and freedom from your pain.

The truth is that Jesus is our Healer, and no amount of pain or brokenness is too far beyond repair.

You are not too broken, damaged, or unclean for the healing and redemptive love of Christ.

Britt

WORTHY
BECAUSE
OF CHRIST

89

When Your Best Isn't Enough

God demonstrates his own love for us in this: While
we were still sinners, Christ died for us.

ROMANS 5:8

I see tons of posts on social media with pretty aesthetics and trendy fonts that tell me I'm worthy and enough.

Any time I see one of these graphics, I raise an eyebrow. That's because I'm painfully acquainted with moments in my life when my best efforts simply *weren't* enough.

Here's the thing: I'm not enough because someone online told me I am. I'm enough because Jesus is enough. He dwells within me, through the finished work of the cross, and I no longer need to try to acquire "enoughness" for myself (thank God!).

As much as I hate to admit it, I'm not perfect, and my best efforts will always come up short. But God knew this would be true for all of us. And He made a plan to bridge the gap of our enoughness. Think about what Romans 5:8 says: "While we were still sinners, Christ died for us." Through His Son, God made a bridge to connect us to Him when our own efforts could never get us there.

I know it feels bleak to think that there's nothing we could ever do to earn our Father's grace. It flies in the face of everything we learn on this earth—the idea that we need to be enough to earn our way to favor. But that's okay! Grace is a gift God gives to us freely when we put our faith in Him (Ephesians 2:8).

So if it were up to me, I'd maybe tweak those posts that I see on social media. Maybe I'd add the phrase "with Him" to the meme. "With Him, I am enough. With Him, I am worthy." Sounds a little better, don't you think?

Cass

I'm not enough because someone online told me I am. I'm enough because Jesus is enough.

90

Staying the Course with Him

Do you not know that in a race all the runners run, but only one gets the prize? Run in such a way as to get the prize. Everyone who competes in the games goes into strict training. They do it to get a crown that will not last, but we do it to get a crown that will last forever.

1 CORINTHIANS 9:24-25

*H*ave you ever run a marathon? If you're anything like me, then your answer is a hard no. I've always been a terrible runner. I have gone through seasons when I enjoyed doing a light jog in the evenings, but I've never run more than a mile at once.

I've always wondered how runners could run more than five miles straight because getting through one mile for me is barely tolerable. I hate having to claw my way to the finish line with tired legs, stinky pits, and thousands of sweat beads running down my face. Just about the only way you could get me to run more than a mile or two, tops, is to put a doughnut at the finish line.

Whenever I see marathon runners, I always admire their focus and perseverance. They have to learn how to pace themselves in order to finish strong. I'm sure that if they were to sprint right away, they'd get worn out quickly and not be able to finish in the time they desired. Or if they wandered off course instead of staying on the path, that surely would delay their arrival to the finish line.

If we see our own lives as a marathon and the path as our walk with God, what happens when we veer off course? Perhaps we get lost. Or maybe we choose another path that leads us away from God.

So how do we know if we're on the wrong path and not on the path God has set before us? Among many things, it might look like:

1. Pleasing people before aiming to please God
2. Living with bitterness
3. Harboring unforgiveness

Don't underestimate what the flesh is capable of when you don't stay close to God. Narrow is the road, friend (Matthew 7:13–14). This means it's not the road that will appeal to most, and walking down it might feel uncomfortable at first. But as iron sharpens iron, your moments of discomfort will sharpen you into the person God wants you to be.

Whatever path you find yourself on today, stay the course with Him. If you've wandered down the wrong path, course correct and walk toward Jesus. Let Him pick you up when you get tired and begin to stumble. Stand firm in your faith, and let nothing deter you away from Him.

Britt

Notes

1. Leo Newhouse, LICSW, "Is Crying Good for You?" Harvard Health, March 1, 2021, https://www.health.harvard.edu/blog/is-crying-good -for-you-2021030122020.
2. Biblehub.com, s. v. "diabolos," https://biblehub.com/greek/1228.htm.
3. Bibletools.org, s. v., "koinonia," accessed October 24, 2022, https://www .bibletools.org/index.cfm/fuseaction/Lexicon.show/ID/G2842/koinonia .htm.
4. *New Oxford American Dictionary*, s. v. "draught."
5. Beth Moore, *Breaking Free: Discover the Victory of Total Surrender* (Nashville: B&H Publishing Group, 2007), 3.
6. Yaqub M., "How Much Counterfeit Money Is In Circulation: The State of Counterfeit Money Statistics (2022 Update)," Renolon.com, October 6, 2022, https://www.renolon.com/counterfeit-money-statistics/.

About the Authors

*B*rittany Maher is compelled by love to empower women to simplify their identity based on one thing alone: *Jesus*. She is the founder of Her True Worth, a large and growing online community designed to liberate an entire generation of faith-filled women with the freedom found in discovering their true worth in Christ. She is also an evangelist with a burning heart for the broken and the lost. She and her husband, Ryan, invest most of their time in equipping and empowering God's people for digital evangelism across the globe. They believe in the importance of using every tool they can to help bring people to a saving knowledge of Jesus. Brittany is planted in Michigan with her husband and their daughter, Ariana.

*C*assandra Speer is a popular Christian blogger whose heart is driven by the desire to see women discover the depth of God's love in a superficial world through the power of His Word. She is vice president of Her True Worth, a ministry created to encourage wounded and wandering women to find their identity and validation in Christ alone. Cassandra is passionate about sharing her faith and tackling the raw and messy moments of life with a little bit of humor—and a whole lot of Jesus! She is also the proud wife of an Air Force veteran. Cassandra and her husband are planted in Oklahoma City, where they live with their three children.

Discover the Woman
You Were Meant to Be

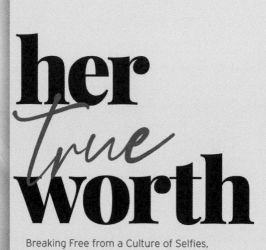

In *Her True Worth*, Brittany Maher and Cassandra Speer deliver a powerful call to women to break free from the bondage of false identities and find their true worth in Jesus Christ.

ISBN: 978-1-4002-3112-6